LOCATION
LONDON

MARK ADAMS

D0346468

First published in 2003 by New Holland Publishers
(UK) Ltd London • Cape Town • Sydney • Auckland

www.newhollandpublishers.com

Garfield House, 86–88 Edgware Road, London W2
2EA, United Kingdom

80 Mckenzie Street, Cape Town 8001, South Africa

14 Aquatic Drive, Frenchs Forest, NSW 2086,
Australia

218 Lake Road, Northcote, Auckland, New Zealand

10 9 8 7 6 5 4 3 2 1

Copyright © 2003 in text: Mark Adams
Copyright © 2003 in photographs as credited below
and on page 176
Copyright © 2003 in maps: Globetrotter™ Travel
Map London (New Holland Publishers)
Copyright © 2003 New Holland Publishers (UK) Ltd

All rights reserved. No part of this publication may
be reproduced, stored in any retrieval system or
transmitted, in any form or by any means,
electronic, mechanical, photocopying, recording or
otherwise, without the prior written permission of
the publishers and copyright holders.

ISBN 1 84330 478 3

Publishing Manager: Jo Hemmings
Senior Editor: Kate Michell
Editor: Sarah Larter
Assistant Editors: Rose Hudson, Jessica Cowie
Cover Design and Design: Gülen Shevki
Production: Joan Woodroffe

Reproduction by Pica Digital Pte Ltd, Singapore
Printed and bound in Singapore by Kyodo Printing
Co. (Singapore) Pte Ltd

Photographs appearing on the cover and prelim
pages are as follows:
Front cover & title page: The River Thames and its
surrounding landmarks, such as St Paul's, are
commonly seen in many movies (David Paterson).
Right: Clive Owen in *Croupier* outside Piccadilly
Circus Underground station (Mark Adams/FilmFour).
Opposite page: Chinatown (David Paterson).

Dedication: For Jake and Charlie

CONTENTS

INTRODUCTION

It is easy to see why London is such a great city for movie locations. What better backdrops are there than Big Ben, Tower Bridge, the Houses of Parliament, St Paul's Cathedral and Trafalgar Square? But, as a city, London offers so much more than these recognizable landmarks to film-makers. There are locations to suit all film genres – period drama, action-adventure, romantic comedy, science-fiction fantasy and even wartime thrills – somewhere in this historic city. London also offers the support structure of great actors and actresses, experienced crews, formidable post-production facilities and some of the best special-effects operations in the world.

For a time, cinematic London seemed to have been reduced to stereotypical images of red double-decker buses and shots of Tower Bridge. While movies that make the most of the city's iconic landmarks clearly have a place, so much more has actually been made of the London buildings and streets over the years.

Before he moved to Hollywood, Alfred Hitchcock located films such as *Sabotage*, *The Man Who Knew Too Much* and *Blackmail* firmly in London. Hitchcock even played with the city's iconic images – blowing up a London bus in *Sabotage* and setting the creepy climax to *Blackmail* in the British Museum. Similarly, the director Michael Powell made the most of the city in films like *Peeping Tom*, while in *Night and the City*, director Jules Dassin presented a stunning film noir vision of London which offered up a frighteningly dark and seedy image of the capital.

Over the years, cinematic London has also been presented in different guises when it has been recreated overseas. The celebrated director G.W. Pabst made his memorable *Die Büchse de Pandora* (*Pandora's Box*) in Germany in 1928; the film starred Louise Brooks and featured a menacing Jack the Ripper character. Foggy streets, plucky bobbies and horse-drawn cabs were the Hollywood trademark of films set in London but shot in Hollywood, such as the 1941 version of *Dr Jekyll and Mr Hyde*, starring Ingrid Bergman and Spencer Tracy, and the Sherlock Holmes movies featuring Basil Rathbone and Nigel Bruce. The classic 1930s musical *Top Hat* was partially set in London and featured a scene in which Fred Astaire drove Ginger Rogers around the city in a hansom cab, all of which was shot in a Hollywood studio. The air raids endured by Greer Garson and Walter Pidgeon in the wartime melodrama *Mrs Miniver* were also studio-based; Covent Garden was recreated in Hollywood for Eliza Doolittle to enjoy a knees-up with her mates in *My Fair Lady*; Julie Andrews as everyone's favourite nanny floated across an artificial London sky in *Mary Poppins* and, more recently, Steven Spielberg's foggy London in the Robin Williams vehicle *Hook* was shot in Los Angeles.

Trafalgar Square is an iconic London landmark in the heart of the city, and as such it is often used as an identifying location in London-set films.

After the Second World War, movie cameras became much easier to handle and location work became far more viable. With the advent of the Swinging Sixties, London became one of the hottest locations for movie backdrops. Both stars and directors wanted to shoot in London because it was the happening place to be. However, although it became physically easier to shoot on location, that didn't necessarily help cut through the stringent red-tape involved with location shooting. When it comes to filming at a major landmark in a capital city, the roads have to be closed down, security has to be in place and film-makers have to play the political game. John Landis managed to get permission to close down Piccadilly Circus for several nights while he set a werewolf rampaging around the streets in *An American Werewolf in London*. Unfortunately, the police and local authorities weren't so happy about the chaos caused by Landis and his werewolf, and for a few years film crews found central London – especially the prime landmarks – almost impossible to access for extensive location filming. Over the years things have gradually changed, and the British Film Commission and the London Film Commission are now in place to help ease negotiations, and these days almost every London borough has a dedicated film officer to help liaise with local officials and police.

In more recent years, several major movies have been filmed in London, ranging from endearing Disney comedies such as *The Parent Trap* and *101 Dalmatians*, through to action-adventures such as *The Mummy Returns*, *Lara Croft: Tomb Raider* and *Mission: Impossible*. While these big-budget movies give the city a major international profile, they go hand-in-hand with numerous other films shot on a broad variety of budgets that have filmed all around London.

Darker and stranger films such as *Repulsion*, *Performance*, *The Servant*, *Blow Up* and *Peeping Tom* offered a different and often more sordid vision of the London streets. At the opposite end of the scale, films such as *Shakespeare in Love*, *Emma*, *Sense and Sensibility*, *The Madness of King George*, *The Golden Bowl*, *Howards End*, and *Maurice* presented a historical vision of the city, from the Elizabethan to the Edwardian era.

A vision of the country during the Thatcher years can be seen in British-made, London-set films such as *The Long Good Friday*, *Naked*, *Mona Lisa* and *High Hopes*, while the typically gloomy (but always amusing) Finn, Aki Kaurismaki, had an equally cynical view of the city in *I Hired a Contract Killer*. However, things change and these days London is very much the city of the romantic comedy; hit titles such as *Four Weddings and a Funeral*, *Notting Hill*, *Bridget Jones's Diary* and *About a Boy*, all of which star London boy Hugh Grant, present the capital as *the* cool place to be when it comes to looking for love.

London is a city with the ability to be all things to all people. From the little-seen cult classic *Death Line* (which features cannibals munching on Underground commuters), through to *Seven Days to Noon* (about a nuclear scientist threatening to blow up London), things don't always go well for London. Equally, classic comedies such as *The Lavender Hill Mob* and *The Ladykillers* show much of that stoical London spirit and ability to laugh in the face of adversity.

The advent of digital technology means that shooting on the city streets is even easier than it has been in days gone by. For Michael Winterbottom shooting *Wonderland* in Soho and beyond, it was simply the case of a man with a small camera using natural light, a few actors and an awful lot of real Londoners. For bigger budget films it is always things like tax breaks, currency rates and star availability that influence where a film is made. The big movies will continue to slug it out with the lower budget projects for shooting space on the London streets for years to come, quite simply because London offers such great backdrops for movies.

Clearly, over the years many films have been made in and around London, and this book cannot hope to cover every single movie shot in the city. I have, however, tried to cover most of the major films made in London, as well as some of the more quirky ones; I have also attempted to deal with most of the key landmark locations, as well as some of the more obscure ones. However, if you know about a film or location that has been omitted, then please do email me at: locationlondon@blueyonder.co.uk

A final question – or maybe a source of debate: What is the best London-set movie? Titles such as *Notting Hill*, *The Ladykillers*, *Alfie*, *The Long Good Friday*, *A Fish Called Wanda*, *Blow Up* and even *Bridget Jones's Diary* might come into contention. My vote goes for the quite wonderful *Passport to Pimlico*… but then maybe that is just the start of the debate down at my local pub…

Mark Adams

A helicopter hovers over Lambeth during the filming of the author's favourite London film, Passport to Pimlico *(1949).*

LOCATION LONDON

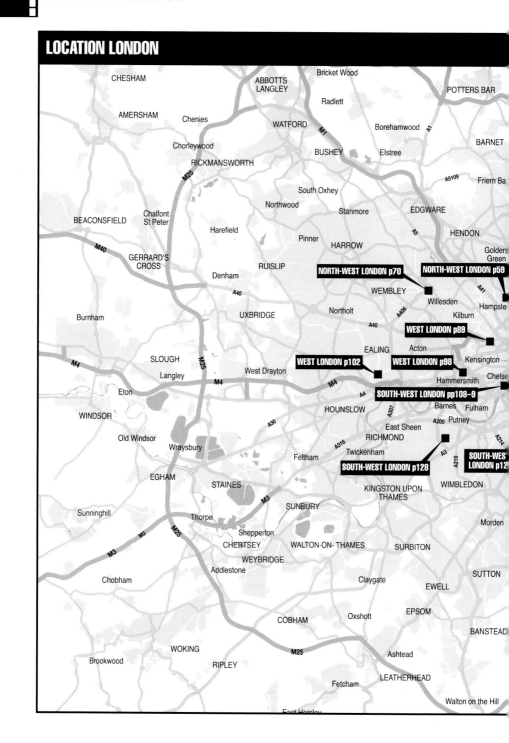

CHESHAM
ABBOTTS LANGLEY
Bricket Wood
POTTERS BAR
Radlett
AMERSHAM
Chenies
WATFORD
Borehamwood
BARNET
Chorleywood
BUSHEY
Elstree
RICKMANSWORTH
A5109
Friern Ba
South Oxhey
Northwood
Stanmore
EDGWARE
BEACONSFIELD
Chalfont St Peter
Harefield
HARROW
HENDON
Golders Green
GERRARD'S CROSS
RUISLIP
Denham
WEMBLEY
NORTH-WEST LONDON p70 **NORTH-WEST LONDON p59**
Willesden
Hampste
Burnham
UXBRIDGE
Northolt
Kilburn
A40
WEST LONDON p89
SLOUGH
West Drayton
EALING
Acton
Kensington
Langley
WEST LONDON p102 **WEST LONDON p98**
Chelse
Eton
Hammersmith
SOUTH-WEST LONDON pp108–9
WINDSOR
HOUNSLOW
Barnes
Fulham
Old Windsor
East Sheen
Putney
Wraysbury
RICHMOND
SOUTH-WES LONDON p12
Feltham
Twickenham
SOUTH-WEST LONDON p128
EGHAM
STAINES
KINGSTON UPON THAMES
WIMBLEDON
Sunninghill
Thorpe
SUNBURY
Morden
Shepperton
CHERTSEY
WALTON-ON- THAMES
SURBITON
WEYBRIDGE
Addlestone
Chobham
Claygate
EWELL
SUTTON
Oxshott
EPSOM
COBHAM
BANSTEAD
WOKING
Ashtead
Brookwood
RIPLEY
LEATHERHEAD
Fetcham
Walton on the Hill
Pinner
AMERSHAM
Beaconsfield
Chalfont

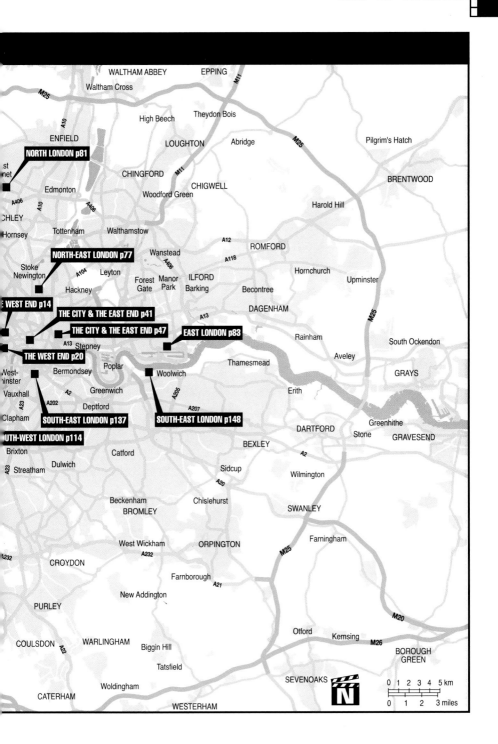

WALTHAM ABBEY   EPPING
Waltham Cross

High Beech   Theydon Bois

ENFIELD   LOUGHTON   Abridge   Pilgrim's Hatch
NORTH LONDON p81
st
net   CHINGFORD   BRENTWOOD
                                          CHIGWELL
Edmonton   Woodford Green
HLEY   Harold Hill
Hornsey   Tottenham   Walthamstow

NORTH-EAST LONDON p77   Wanstead   ROMFORD
Stoke   Hornchurch
Newington   Leyton   Upminster
                    Forest Manor   ILFORD
Hackney   Gate   Park   Barking   Becontree
WEST END p14   DAGENHAM
THE CITY & THE EAST END p41
THE CITY & THE EAST END p47
                                    EAST LONDON p83
A13   Stepney   Rainham   South Ockenden
THE WEST END p20
West-   Bermondsey   Poplar   Thamesmead   Aveley
inster   Woolwich   GRAYS
Vauxhall   Greenwich   Erith
Clapham   Deptford   A207
SOUTH-EAST LONDON p137   SOUTH-EAST LONDON p148   Greenhithe
                                    DARTFORD   Stone   GRAVESEND
UTH-WEST LONDON p114   BEXLEY
Brixton   Catford
Streatham   Dulwich   Sidcup   Wilmington

Beckenham   Chislehurst   SWANLEY
BROMLEY

West Wickham   ORPINGTON   Farningham
CROYDON

Farnborough
New Addington
PURLEY
                                                M20
                        Otford   Kemsing   M26
COULSDON   WARLINGHAM   Biggin Hill   BOROUGH
                                          GREEN
Tatsfield
SEVENOAKS
Woldingham   0 1 2 3 4 5 km
CATERHAM
WESTERHAM   0 1   2   3 miles

THE WEST END

Making movies in the West End can be both a dream and a nightmare for film-makers. Britain's capital has a wonderful selection of stunning backdrops that provide scale and grandeur to any given scene – think how frequently London icons such as Leicester Square, the British Museum and Trafalgar Square have appeared in films. However, the logistics and red tape involved in filming in such well-known spots cause huge headaches. Despite such difficulties, film-makers have managed to make wonderful use of some of central London's most recognizable features over the years, from Ancient Egyptian mummies escaping from the British Museum in **The Mummy Returns** (2001) to Hugh Grant speeding through the city's busy streets to the Savoy Hotel to declare his undying love to Julia Roberts in **Notting Hill** (1999).

The impressive Empire cinema in the heart of Leicester Square has been the location for many movie premières, including the fictitious one attended by Hugh Grant and Julia Roberts in *Notting Hill* (1999).

BLOOMSBURY

Bloomsbury is an area redolent of everything artistic and academic. Home to the magnificent British Museum and one of Britain's most prestigious places of learning, University College, London, it is an area that gave its name to the Bloomsbury set, which comprised some of the most influential artists and writers of the early 20th century, including Virginia Woolf and E.M. Forster.

British Museum

The British Museum is a Bloomsbury venue that works extremely well in the movies, and has continued to perform as a location over many years. In **Blackmail** (1929), Alfred Hitchcock's first sound film, the finale was set in the museum, with Hitchcock making clever use of trick photography and expressionist visuals as the villain is chased over the roof of the building. In Jacques Tourneur's devil-cult chiller **Night of the Demon** (1957), which was based on the M.R. James short story *Casting the Runes* and starred Dana Andrews and Peggy Cummins, a supernatural force manifests itself in the museum's reading room.

Alfred Hitchcock used the atmospheric British Museum for the backdrop of his first sound film, Blackmail *(1929).*

The British Museum has featured in many films, ranging from Night of the Demon *(1957) to* The Mummy Returns *(2001).*

In Fred Zinnemann's **The Day of the Jackal** (1973), a professional hitman (Edward Fox) hired to assassinate General de Gaulle does a little research in the old circular reading room of the British Museum library. **Isadora** (1968), directed by Karel Reisz and starring Vanessa Redgrave as the unconventional dancer Isadora Duncan, sees the character entranced by the Elgin Marbles in a visit to the museum. The marbles also entrance Mo (played by Jane Horrocks) in the romantic comedy **Born Romantic** (2000). Scenes from James Ivory's drama **Maurice** (1987) made particular use of the Assyrian Salon. Gregory Peck and Sophia Loren also paid the building a visit for scenes in the comedy thriller **Arabesque** (1966), directed by Hollywood veteran Stanley Donen.

The British Museum has a key role in Neil LaBute's **Possession** (2002), which stars Gwyneth Paltrow and Aaron Eckhart. The film is based on A.S. Byatt's 1990 Booker Prize-winning novel of the same name. In the film, Paltrow and Eckhart play Maud Bailey and Roland Michell, a pair of contemporary literary investigators researching the secrets of two Victorian poets (played by Jeremy Northam and Jennifer Ehle). The modern couple soon find themselves falling under the spell of the passionate story of the Victorian lovers. *Possession* became the first film to shoot in the museum during opening hours, as well as in non-public areas that have

'We were very lucky to have access to so many parts of the British Museum... they reek of academic atmosphere.'

SUE QUINN, LOCATION MANAGER, *POSSESSION*

never been seen on film before. The film's location manager, Sue Quinn, said: 'We were very lucky to have access to so many parts of the British Museum since they are absolutely perfect for this particular story – they reek of academic atmosphere.' Actor Aaron Eckhart added: 'Working at the British Museum was truly inspirational – especially working around the artefacts.'

Not surprisingly, given some of the Egyptian relics on display at the museum, a lot of films feature the revival of the dead. In Mike Newell's **The Awakening** (1980), an adaptation of Bram Stoker's *The Jewel of Seven Stars* (which had previously served for the basis of the 1971 Hammer film *Blood from the Mummy's Tomb*), Charlton Heston awakens an evil princess in the museum's Hall of Egyptian Antiquities. The exteriors of the museum were actually shot nearby at University College on Gower Street, with interiors built in the studio.

More recently, in Stephen Sommers' **The Mummy Returns** (2001), which stars Brendan Fraser and Rachel Weisz, the film's bad guys set about reviving an evil mummy (Arnold Vosloo) at the museum. In this case the museum was largely recreated at a studio, though the escape sequences, in which a quartet of evil mummies chase the heroes (who just happen to be on board a red double-decker bus) were filmed outside the British Museum. Once again, however, nearby University College stood in for the museum in some key exterior shots.

THE WEST END

KEY
1. Blackmail (1929)
2. Night of the Demon (1957)
3. The Day of the Jackal (1973)
4. Isadora (1968)
5. Maurice (1987)
6. Arabesque (1966)
7. Possession (2002)
8. The Awakening (1980)
9. The Mummy Returns (2001)
10. Doctor in the House (1954)
11. The Hunger (1983)

Gower Street

As well as standing in for the British Museum, University College, which has many buildings in Gower Street and the surrounding area, has also doubled as a hospital in **Doctor in the House** (1954). Directed by Ralph Thomas, this was the first in the series of films based on Richard Gordon's 'Doctor' books. The college functioned as the exterior of St Swithin's Hospital, the playground and supposed learning place of a band of young doctors led by Dirk Bogarde, Donald Sinden and Kenneth More. Senate House, the university's library in Malet Street to the south of the main entrance, has also featured in films. In the vampire flick **The Hunger** (1983), starring David Bowie and Catherine Deneuve, it appeared as a New York clinic, while in the fine 1995 adaptation of Shakespeare's historical tragedy *Richard III,* which starred Ian McKellen in the title role, it served as the king's bunker.

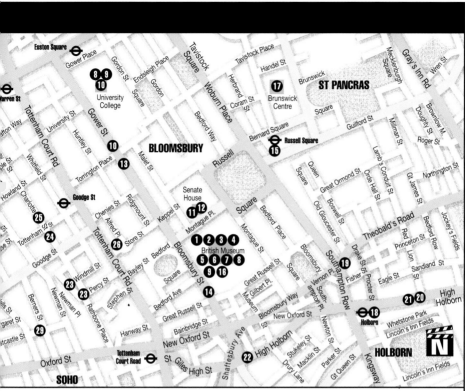

12. Richard III (1995)
13. Stage Fright (1950)
14. Shirley Valentine (1989)
15. Death Line (1974)
16. Bulldog Jack (1935)
17. The Passenger (1975)

18. Secrets and Lies (1996)
19. The Avengers (1998)
20. Howards End (1992)
21. Jude (1996)
22. I Believe in You (1952)
23. Peeping Tom (1960)

24. A Hard Day's Night (1966)
25. Sliding Doors (1998)
26. Hidden City (1987)
27. Bedazzled (1967)
28. Death at Broadcasting House (1934)
29. Eyes Wide Shut (1998)

At 62–64 Gower Street the Royal Academy of Dramatic Art (RADA) can be found. This most eminent of drama schools was used in a scene from Sir Alfred Hitchcock's **Stage Fright** (1950). Jane Wyman was Eve, a young RADA student who takes on a

Dirk Bogarde (second from right) and fellow medical students in the classic *Doctor in the House (1954).*

detective role to try and track down a murderer. Richard Todd plays her former boyfriend, Jonathan Cooper, who is accused of the crime, while Marlene Dietrich appears as Charlotte Inwood, a singing star. In one scene, Cooper evades the police by hiding out at one of Eve's classes at the school.

It is the Marlborough Hotel on Bloomsbury Street, which runs on from Gower Street, where bored Liverpool housewife Shirley (Pauline Collins) goes with her old school friend Marjorie (Joanna Lumley) for tea in **Shirley Valentine** (1989). Revelations ensue as we discover that Marjorie's career path has taken her into high-class prostitution.

Russell Square

North of the British Museum is Russell Square tube station, whose exterior and interior served as a location for one of the most underrated British horror films, **Death Line** (1974), which was directed by Gary Sherman. The opening scene, which takes place on the station platform, sees a bowler-hatted city gent abducted by a misshapen cannibal that has been lurking in the Underground system. The story is based on a classic London urban myth about a gang of workers who were supposedly trapped during the building of the British Museum tube station in the 19th century (the station was subsequently closed in 1933). The ingenious film, which stars Donald Pleasence and Christopher Lee, suggests that the workers survived the disaster and lurk in the closed station, having been transformed into man-eating monsters that snack on commuters.

The closure of the British Museum station also helped inspire the comedy crime drama **Bulldog Jack** (1935), an engaging spoof of the 'Bulldog Drummond' detective stories that were popular in the 1920s. Brothers Jack and Claude Hulbert (as Jack Pennington and Algy Longworth) track down an evil mastermind (Ralph Richardson) to the fictitious abandoned Bloomsbury Station (all built on a studio set), and manage to rescue Ann Manders (played by *King Kong* star Fay Wray) along the way.

Almost opposite Russell Square tube station is the Brunswick Centre, home to the art house Renoir cinema. The centre features in cult Italian director Michelangelo Antonioni's globe-trotting drama **The Passenger** (1975). In the film, Jack Nicholson (playing burnt-out television reporter David Locke) steals a passport and assumes the identity of a dead man, who also happens to be a gun runner. Early sections of the film were shot at the Brunswick Centre, before Nicholson's character heads off to Germany, Chad and Spain.

HOLBORN

In Mike Leigh's superlative **Secrets and Lies** (1996), the moving scene where Cynthia (Brenda Blethyn) and Hortense (Marianne Jean-Baptiste) meet in a coffee shop and discover they are actually mother and daughter was shot at a coffee bar near to Holborn tube station. Both actresses received deserved Oscar nominations for their performances. The big-screen version of **The Avengers** (1998) shot at a number of London locations, including the disused Kingsway Tram Tunnel in Holborn, in the scene where Steed (Ralph Fiennes) and Mrs Peel (Uma Thurman) drive down the tunnel for a meeting at 'The Ministry'.

The Merchant Ivory costume drama **Howards End** (1992) also made use of the area. Scenes of the Porphyrion Insurance Company, where Leonard Bast (Samuel West) initially has a job, were shot at the Pearl Insurance Building, High Holborn, with the exterior doubling as the company run in the film by Henry Wilcox (Anthony Hopkins). The Pearl Insurance building was also used by director Michael Winterbottom in **Jude** (1996), which was based on Thomas Hardy's tragic novel *Jude the Obscure*. The film featured Christopher Eccleston in the title role, with Kate Winslet as his lover Sue Bridehead.

The original Oasis Swimming Pool in Holborn was created from the cellars of a bombed-out building and can be seen in the drama **I Believe in You** (1952), in scenes of a young Joan Collins, who plays underprivileged Norma, taking a dip with Hooker (Harry Fowler). The swimming pool has since been rebuilt and now stands on the corner of High Holborn and Endell Street.

FITZROVIA

Michael Powell's dark masterpiece **Peeping Tom** (1960) opens in Fitzrovia, an area north of Oxford Street and west of Tottenham Court Road. As the film begins we see the deeply disturbed Mark (Carl Boehm) picking up a prostitute (Brenda Bruce), who is lurking close to the Newman Arms pub at 23 Rathbone Street. Powell, who shoots partially from the point of view of a hand-held camera, follows her as she walks down the cobbled Newman Passage (next to the pub), into a doorway and up to her flat

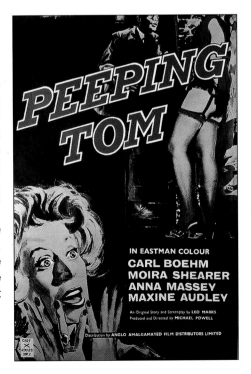

Michael Powell's controversial Peeping Tom *(1960) painted a seedy picture of London's Fitzrovia area.*

(though in reality this would take you to the pub's upstairs rooms) where Mark kills her. The scenes of Mark taking his scooter to a seedy newsagent where businessmen buy pornographic photographs were shot just a few yards away from Newman Passage at the shop – which is still a newsagent – at the corner of Percy Street and Rathbone Place. Filming also took place in Holland Park.

The concert scenes in the excellent musical-romp **A Hard Day's Night** (1966), starring The Beatles, were shot at the old Scala Theatre. Now long gone, it was on Charlotte Street, a road that runs parallel to Tottenham Court Road, and you can still spot the alleyway from which the Fab Four emerged to make it to the concert. The exterior fire escape scenes were, however, filmed at the Hammersmith Odeon in West London. The Scala also doubled as the television studio in which the band practises and performs the film's climactic televised concert. Charlotte Street and its environs is a busy spot for film industry types, with various film companies based there, and its many restaurants are popular with industry folk.

At 19 Charlotte Street is Bertorelli's restaurant and bar, which was used extensively in Peter Howitt's romantic comedy **Sliding Doors** (1998). This intriguing film offers two possible lives for Helen Quilley (Gwyneth Paltrow) after she loses her job. In one she drowns her sorrows in Bertorelli's bar, but in another version of her life she gets a job as a waitress in the restaurant.

Stephen Poliakoff's debut as a writer-director **Hidden City** (1987) starred Charles Dance as James Richards, a sociologist who digs into government secrets in a series of vaults beneath London. This fascinating film was shot partly at Security Archives at the Eisenhower Centre, located just off Tottenham Court Road. The film also starred Cassie Stuart and Bill Paterson.

Forget the recent re-make of *Bedazzled* (2001) starring Elizabeth Hurley – rather search out the wonderful Stanley Donen original, starring Peter Cook as the devil (or George Spiggot as he is called) and Dudley Moore as Stanley Moon, the mild-mannered man he intends to corrupt. This **Bedazzled** (1967) is a classic from the 1960s, featuring a bikini-clad Raquel Welch as Lillian Lust and – just as memorably – nuns on trampolines. London-shot scenes include Cook and Moore on top of one of the architectural icons of the 1960s, the Post Office Tower, with Cook sending off a pigeon to deposit an unwelcome gift on a businessman's hat.

The British Film Institute (BFI) is based at 21 Stephen Street, just off Tottenham Court Road. It houses the BFI's extensive library, thought to be the world's largest collection of documentation on film and television. The BFI's information service and various other departments are also housed at the offices.

Portland Place

Just north of Oxford Circus, at Portland Place, is Broadcasting House, the famous home of the BBC's radio operations, and also the setting for a classic British mystery drama, titled – imaginatively enough – **Death at Broadcasting House** (1934). Though largely studio-based, the distinctive building can still be seen in Reginald Denham's enjoyable film, which stars Ian Hunter, Austin Trevor and Mary Newland.

COVENT GARDEN

The former Covent Garden market is now a popular and crowded shopping area, with street entertainers where flower girls, such as *My Fair Lady*'s Eliza Doolittle, once plied their trade. Ironically, the movie version of *My Fair Lady* (1964) recreated Covent Garden in a studio.

It is in the old Covent Garden – when it was still a flower, fruit and vegetable market – that many early scenes of Alfred Hitchcock's chiller **Frenzy** (1972) were shot. The film, about a murderer causing mayhem in London, was Hitchcock's penultimate film, and marked a brief return to his London roots. Jon Finch plays the main suspect, and in The Globe pub on Bow Street he overhears a conversation about the killings.

In the hit comedy **Four Weddings and a Funeral** (1994), the characters played by Hugh Grant and Andie MacDowell have a conversation in a restaurant where they recount memories of their various lovers. This was shot at the Dôme restaurant on Wellington Street.

Andie MacDowell and Hugh Grant relax outside Covent Garden's Dôme restaurant, where a scene was shot for the box-office hit Four Weddings and a Funeral *(1994).*

THE WEST END

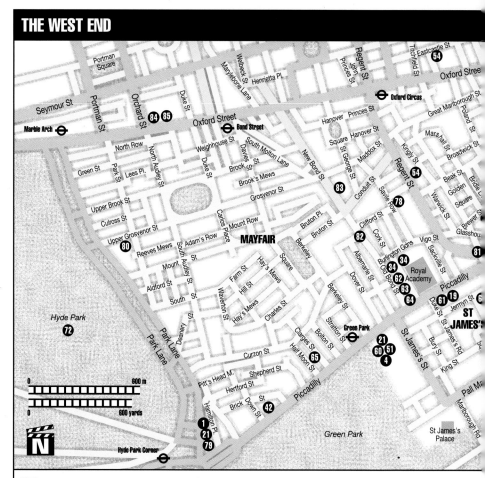

KEY

1. A Hard Day's Night (1966)
2. Frenzy (1972)
3. Four Weddings and a Funeral (1994)
4. Modesty Blaise (1966)
5. The Red Shoes (1948)
6. Travels with my Aunt (1972)
7. Victim (1961)
8. Billy Elliott (2000)
9. Killing me Softly (2001)
10. Shanghai Knights (2002)
11. Johnny English (2002)
12. Another Life (1999)
13. Harry Potter and the Philosopher's Stone (2001)
14. Shining Through (1992)
15. Superman IV: The Quest for Peace (1987)
16. An American Werewolf in London (1981)
17. Patriot Games (1992)
18. The Duellists (1977)
19. Howards End (1992)
20. Sabotage (1936)
21. Notting Hill (1999)
22. The Long Good Friday (1980)
23. Entrapment (1999)
24. The Day of the Jackal (1973)
25. GoldenEye (1995)
26. Tomorrow Never Dies (1997)
27. Sleepy Hollow (1999)
28. Sense and Sensibility (1995)
29. Wilde (1998)
30. The Secret Agent (1995)
31. Black Beauty (1994)
32. Reds (1981)
33. The Hunger (1983)
34. 101 Dalmatians (1996)
35. Arabesque (1966)
36. Honest (2000)
37. The Day the Earth Caught Fire (1961)
38. It Happened Here (1964)
39. The Avengers (1998)
40. Miranda (2002)
41. Enigma (2001)

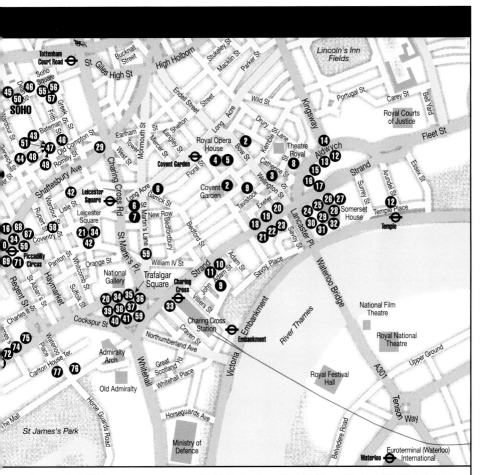

42. Gangster No. 1 (2000)
43. Eskimo Nell (1975)
44. The Playbirds (1978)
45. Emanuelle in Soho (1981)
46. Wonderland (1998)
47. The Tommy Steele Story (1957)
48. Expresso Bongo (1959)
49. The Rebel (1960)
50. Beat Girl (1962)
51. Mona Lisa (1986)
52. Naked (1993)
53. Bring me the Head of Mavis Davis (1999)
54. Eyes Wide Shut (1999)
55. Blue Ice (1992)
56. Melody (aka S.W.A.L.K.) (1971)

57. 84 Charing Cross Road (1987)
58. About a Boy (2002)
59. Night and the City (1950)
60. Dinner at the Ritz (1937)
61. Darling (1965)
62. Patriot Games (1992)
63. Tom & Viv (1994)
64. Incognito (1997)
65. Half Moon Street (1986)
66. The Jokers (1967)
67. Croupier (1999)
68. Brannigan (1975)
69. The Day of the Triffids (1962)
70. Bedazzled (1967)
71. Bend it Like Beckham (2002)

72. Around the World in Eighty
    Days (1956)
73. The Avengers (1998)
74. The Man Who Cried (2000)
75. The Last Minute (2000)
76. Bridget Jones's Diary (2001)
77. The Wings of the Dove (1991)
78. Let it Be (1970)
79. Dr No (1962)
80. Sexy Beast (2000)
81. Maurice (1987)
82. Help! (1965)
83. Octopussy (1983)
84. Love on Wheels (1932)
85. Taxi for Two (1929)

The popular Lamb and Flag pub, on the edge of Covent Garden, was a location for George Cukor's Travels with my Aunt *(1972).*

The wonderfully kitsch but rarely seen **Modesty Blaise** (1966), directed by Joseph Losey, shot scenes all around the world, including in London. Blaise was a popular character in comic strips and books – a female James Bond with a sexy male sidekick. Italian actress Monica Vitti played the title character, with Terence Stamp playing her accomplice Willie Garvin. In the film, Blaise is lured out of retirement by British spy chief Sir Gerald Tarrant (Harry Andrews) while attending a performance at the Royal Opera House in Covent Garden.

The Royal Opera House is also the location for the opening scenes of Michael Powell and Emeric Pressburger's enchanting and innovative classic **The Red Shoes** (1948), which told the story of a ballerina, Victoria Page (Moira Shearer), who has to choose between her lover and her career. The film then promptly switches location to a series of spots in France and Monte Carlo.

The Lamb and Flag pub in Rose Street provides one of the scenes in George Cukor's comedy **Travels With My Aunt** (1972), an adaptation of a Graham Greene novel. It starred Maggie Smith as the 'aunt' and Alec McCowen as mild-mannered bank manager Henry Pulling. Smith's London flat in the film is also located nearby, above the Salisbury pub in St Martin's Lane. The Salisbury also crops up in Basil Dearden's **Victim** (1961), starring Dirk Bogarde, Sylvia Syms and Peter McEnery, in a plot that dealt with a bisexual barrister who was being blackmailed.

Although the majority of the endearing comedy-drama **Billy Elliott** (2000) was shot in the north of England, the end of Stephen Daldry's film sees Billy's father (Gary Lewis) and brother Tom (Jamie Draven) heading down to London to see him perform in *Swan Lake*. The theatre they arrive at – late – is the Theatre Royal, Drury Lane.

STRAND

The erotic-thriller **Killing Me Softly** (2001) looked perfect on paper, which is where – of course – it had its origin. Based on the bestseller by Nicci French (in reality the

'**S**o many of the films you see set in London look dark and moody. I wanted to show the vibrant, active side of London. It is a city full of energy.'

CHEN KAIGE, DIRECTOR,
KILLING ME SOFTLY

husband-and-wife writing team of Sean French and Nicci Gerrard), the film marked the English-language debut of acclaimed Chinese director Chen Kaige, and starred Heather Graham and Joseph Fiennes. Unfortunately, it had some of the worst reviews ever bestowed on a film.

Shot in London (with a few locations in Cumbria) in late 2000, the film is the steamy tale of a UK-based American woman, Alice (Graham) who embarks on a passionate affair with a hunky mountaineer, Adam (Fiennes). However, she soon begins to wonder if he is actually a killer. Much of the filming took place around the Strand, especially at the Adelphi Building, and on John Adam Street, towards the river. Alice gets her first glimpse of Adam as they stand waiting at a zebra crossing on the Strand.

Chen Kaige said: 'Making my first English language film in London is an added challenge, because I knew nothing about the city, but I was very curious. London is obviously international and more obviously multi-cultural than Los Angeles.'

Also shot at John Adam Street, just behind the Strand, were some scenes from the comedy-adventure **Shanghai Knights** (2002), as were elements of the spy spoof **Johnny English** (2002), directed by Peter Howitt. The latter film stars Rowan Atkinson as blundering spy Johnny English (based on the character he played in the series of television adverts for Barclaycard), with John Malkovich and Natalie Imbruglia. The film shot at the Royal Society of Arts (RSA) on John Adam Street.

The Waldorf Hotel, on Aldwych, featured in Philip Goodhew's period drama **Another Life** (1999), starring Natasha Little and Ioan Gruffudd. Shooting also took place at Temple Place. The nearby Australian High Commission, with its bold archways, marble decor and glittering chandeliers, made the perfect location for Gringotts Wizarding Bank in **Harry Potter and the Philosopher's Stone** (US title: **Harry Potter and the Sorcerer's Stone** 2001). But once news got out that the Commission had been used as a location in the phenomenally successful film, guided tours around the

The elegant Savoy Hotel on the Strand has been used in several films.

wonderful building had to be suspended as it wasn't equipped to deal with a tourist invasion.

In **Shining Through** (1992), Aldwych and Kingsway stood in for New York. While the abandoned Aldwych tube station doubled as the New York underground in **Superman IV: The Quest for Peace** (1987), easily the worst film in the Superman series, but at least reuniting the main leads of Christopher Reeve, Gene Hackman and Margot Kidder. The station also features in **An American Werewolf in London** (1981) and **Patriot Games** (1992).

The restaurant Simpson's-in-the-Strand, renowned for its traditional English fare, was used for certain interior scenes in Ridley Scott's debut film **The Duellists** (1977), which starred Keith Carradine and Harvey Keitel as two rival officers who fight a series of duels during the Napoleonic Wars. Simpson's can also be seen in **Howards End** (1992) in a scene where Henry Wilcox (Anthony Hopkins) and Margaret Schlegel (Emma Thompson) meet for lunch. In Alfred Hitchcock's **Sabotage** (1936), Sylvia Verloc (Sylvia Sydney), who is married to the film's saboteur, meets undercover policeman Sergeant Ted Spencer (John Loder) at Trafalgar Square before moving on to Simpson's for a meal. The meal itself, though, was shot in the studio. The final scene, in which a bomb explodes on a London bus, is supposedly set on the Strand, but it was shot at a studio.

The Savoy Hotel on the Strand has a key role in the romantic comedy **Notting Hill** (1999), as it is the location for the film's climax. As the film builds to its peak, William (Hugh Grant) dashes across London to try and track Anna (Julia Roberts) down before she returns to the US. He finally finds her and declares his love, and – naturally enough – she responds in kind. The Savoy can also be seen in scenes towards the end of the great British crime film **The Long Good Friday** (1980). Harold Shand (Bob Hoskins) is a London mobster trying to raise Mafia money to invest in the up-and-coming Docklands area. His Mafia contacts stay at the Savoy, and near the end of the film Shand is kidnapped from the hotel. Worth looking out for in the film is a young Pierce Brosnan playing an IRA man.

Sean Connery also makes a brief visit to the Savoy in **Entrapment** (1999). He plays a daring jewel thief, Robert 'Mac' MacDougal, who is pursued by an insurance agent (Catherine Zeta Jones). After initial scenes in New York, the film switches to London, and, following the obligatory establishing shot of the River Thames, Big Ben etc., the scene switches to the Savoy. Beneath the hotel's famous art deco sign Mac gets into a black cab and heads into the City, with the insurance agent in hot pursuit.

Somerset House, on the Strand close to Waterloo Bridge, is where all records of births, deaths and marriages were once held, and regularly crops up in movies. In **The Day of the Jackal** (1973), the assassin played by Edward Fox goes there to furnish himself with a false birth certificate. Somerset House has also featured in **GoldenEye** (1995), in which it doubled as a St Petersburg location in a scene where Joe Don Baker tries to fix his Russian car; the same location also appeared in a subsequent Bond film, **Tomorrow Never Dies** (1997), as MI6 headquarters.

The courtyard of Somerset House doubled as a turn-of-the-century New York

Somerset House on the Embankment has doubled as locations as varied as St Petersburg and early 20th-century New York.

location in Tim Burton's gothic thriller **Sleepy Hollow** (1999), which starred Johnny Depp, and was also used in Ang Lee's wonderful adaptation of Jane Austen's **Sense and Sensibility** (1995), starring Emma Thompson and Kate Winslet. In **Wilde** (1998) Somerset House was used to double as the exterior of the writer's plush London apartment. It was also used as a location for **The Secret Agent** (1995), with Bob Hoskins, and Caroline Thompson's engaging updating of the classic **Black Beauty** (1994), which featured Sean Bean and David Thewlis. Meanwhile in Warren Beatty's epic **Reds** (1981) Somerset House stood in for a Russian building attacked by Bolshevik revolutionaries.

The nightclub Heaven, at the other end of the Strand, towards Trafalgar Square, is situated underneath the arches at Charing Cross Station and doubled as a New York nightclub for Tony Scott's stylish vampire film **The Hunger** (1983).

TRAFALGAR SQUARE

Movies often make use of Trafalgar Square, with Nelson's Column, the impressive sculptured lions and the fountains. In **101 Dalmatians** (1996) Anita (Joely Richardson) cycles through the square with her Dalmatian, while in the comedy thriller **Arabesque** (1966) director Stanley Donen managed to get permission to raise a camera to the top of Nelson's Column using a block and tackle.

The ever-popular Trafalgar Square regularly turns up as a movie backdrop.

A crime comedy set in swinging London of the late 1960s, **Honest** (2000) attracted much publicity (though eventually poor reviews) mainly due to the fact that it starred three of the four members of hot all-girl singing group All Saints. The All Saints girls – the Appleton sisters (Nicole and Natalie) and Melanie Blatt – play the three streetwise Chase sisters from the East End who head 'up West' with robbery on their minds. The girls start thieving, with their faces hidden by iconic masks, and begin to challenge not only the law, but also the 'old boy' code of the East London underworld gangs. In keeping with the music business association, *Honest* also marked the directorial debut of Eurythmics star David A. Stewart. The film shot in and around London – making especially good use of Trafalgar Square and Lincoln's Inn – as well as taking a brief trip to Oxford to shoot certain sequences.

In **The Day the Earth Caught Fire** (1961), a sci-fi film directed by Val Guest, a CND rally was shot in Trafalgar Square. At the other end of the political spectrum, in Kevin Brownlow's impressive and chilling **It Happened Here** (1964), which deals with what might have happened had Germany successfully invaded Britain, a Nazi rally is held there.

Thanks to the wizardry of special effects, Trafalgar Square is covered with snow in **The Avengers** (1998). As the evil Father (Fiona Shaw) and the evil double for Mrs Peel (Uma Thurman) attempt to make their escape by balloon they crash into a sign next to Trafalgar Square, while the real Mrs Peel falls from the balloon into snow next to Nelson's Column. An empty Trafalgar Square can be seen in the chiller **28 Days Later** (2002) directed by Danny Boyle.

Trafalgar Square is also used as a backdrop for the contemporary drama **Miranda** (2002), directed by Marc Munden and starring Christina Ricci as a woman with multiple personalities. In the film, John Simm plays an innocent Yorkshire librarian who falls for Miranda, whose personalities include a geisha, con-woman, businesswoman, dominatrix and dancer. Trafalgar Square and the nearby Adelphi Hotel featured in scenes from the drama **Enigma** (2001), which was based on Robert Harris's bestseller and directed by Michael Apted. The film dealt with a mystery involving spies and murder at Bletchley Park, the home of war-time code-breakers, and starred Kate Winslet, Dougray Scott and Saffron Burrows.

LEICESTER SQUARE

Leicester Square is very much the heart of London's film world, with three of its four sides containing some of the biggest and best of London's cinema screens. The majestic Odeon Leicester Square, built on the site of the old Alhambra Music Hall, opened as a cinema in November 1937 and was the flagship of the Oscar Deutsch cinema chain. The interior featured leopard-skin patterned material on the seating (which has been restored), naked figures leaping from the walls, and a mighty organ that rose from the stage. The cinema was damaged during the Second World War, but was subsequently repaired and has gone on to be the key venue for any major film première in London. Also in Leicester Square are the two-screen Odeon West End and the multi-screen Warner West End. The Empire, on the north side of Leicester Square, was used in the film **Notting Hill** (1999) as the location for a scene towards the end of the film in which the characters played by Hugh Grant and Julia Roberts attend a black-tie première of a new movie. Within a half-mile radius of Leicester Square are numerous other cinemas.

The British crime film **Gangster No. 1** (2000), starring Paul Bettany and Malcolm McDowell, shot a crucial nightclub scene at the once-glamorous club Café de Paris in Leicester Square. The film also shot in Chinatown, north of Leicester Square.

Paul Bettany plays the gun-wielding ambitious mobster in Gangster No. 1 *(2000).*

'There's plenty of gold in the Café de Paris, but we put more in and re-dressed it until it came across as an authentic 1960s nightclub,'

RICHARD BRIDGLAND,
PRODUCTION DESIGNER,
GANGSTER NO. 1

The area around Leicester Square makes an appearance in a scene from **101 Dalmatians** (1996). Jeff Daniels plays Roger, a computer artist and proud owner of a Dalmatian named Pongo, while Joely Richardson plays Anita, a fashion designer, and owner of another of the dogs. We see the characters cycling through London, via plenty of landmarks. They take in sites including Leicester Square, Trafalgar Square, Piccadilly Circus and Burlington Arcade, before (literally) bumping into each other in Battersea Park.

SOHO

As one might imagine, Soho is one of those areas of London much loved by film-makers. Not only do they tend to know the area extremely well – most of them hang out at the private clubs in the area, such as the Groucho, Black's, Union or Soho House, or are regulars in the local pubs – but this small part of London has a certain bohemian reputation tinged with seediness that suits the movie industry.

There is a whole raft of horror films set in Soho whose cameras never even came near the British shores, let alone made it to London. Movies such as the German-made *The Phantom of Soho* (aka *Das Phantom von Soho*) (1964), *The Gorilla of Soho* (*Der Gorilla von Soho*) (1968) and *The Hunchback of Soho* (*Der Bucklige von Soho*) (1966) were all shot elsewhere in the world, while Germany played host to *The Monster of London City* (*Das Ungeheuer von London City*) (1964), and Hungary was the base for *Edge of Sanity* (1989), about a Soho-based Dr Jekyll character (Anthony Hopkins). The somewhat tawdry background of the area has also lent itself to crime films – again not actually shot there – such as *Murder in Soho* (1939).

Of course, the seedier side of Soho – that of red lights and sex shops – does appear as a theme in some movies. The sex comedy **Eskimo Nell** (1975), directed by Martin Campbell – who went on to find greater directorial fame with *GoldenEye* (1995) and *The Mask of Zorro* (1998) – offers an often amusing look at British soft-porn of the 1970s, and contains scenes shot in a variety of Soho preview theatres and distribution company offices. Scenes from **The Playbirds** (1978) were shot at the notorious Raymond Revuebar, just off Brewer Street. Also partially shot in Soho – as is suggested by the title – was **Emmanuelle in Soho** (1981).

Wilde (1998), in which Stephen Fry gave a remarkable performance in the title role, used the exterior of the Palace Theatre at Cambridge Circus, where Old

The seedier side of Soho, including the famous Raymond Revuebar, has featured in numerous films over the years.

Compton Street joins Charing Cross Road, for the scene showing the opening of Wilde's play *Lady Windermere's Fan*.

In **Wonderland** (1998), an acclaimed drama which starred Gina McKee, director Michael Winterbottom went out onto the streets of Soho to film the interweaving story of three sisters and their relationships, using hand-held cameras, a reduced crew and natural lighting. Winterbottom said: 'Because of the way we decided to film, we shot everything in what we felt was the "real" location. For example, in the script Nadia (McKee) worked in a café in Soho. Now, often when you make a film, you might shoot that café somewhere else just to make it easier. But on *Wonderland* we always shot in real places – so her café is on Old Compton Street.

'What's more, because we shot in real locations, without extras and when places were open, we had to shoot at the same time as the events were happening. For example, the opening scene of the film takes place in the Pitcher and Piano bar in Soho (on Dean Street). Normally, a film would take over a location like that, close it down, fill it with extras and probably shoot a night scene at ten o'clock in the morning. For us to get that "end of the night" scene we had to wait until the end of the night, wait until everyone was drunk and ready to go home, before we could get the right atmosphere.'

Studio-set films, such as the musicals **The Tommy Steele Story** (1957) and **Expresso Bongo** (1959), which starred Cliff Richard and Laurence Harvey, and the Tony Hancock comedy **The Rebel** (1960), partly set themselves in the hip Old

Compton Street coffee bars of the late 1950s, while the road also appears in the cult movie **Beat Girl** (1962), an attempt to launch pop singer Adam Faith as the British answer to Elvis Presley. The film included street drag racing, beatnik parties and sessions in a Soho strip club. The club in the film is located on Old Compton Street, and is run by a sleazy-looking Christopher Lee. Old Compton Street is also the address of the private club in the crime drama **Mona Lisa** (1986) that is visited by George (Bob Hoskins). In Mike Leigh's searing drama **Naked** (1993), the scene where Johnny (David Thewlis) meets the foul-mouthed Scottish oddball Archie (Ewan Bremner) was shot in the doorway of the shop Lina Stores, at 18 Brewer Street. Further along Brewer Street, towards Regent Street is the trendy Atlantic Bar and Grill, where the comedy-drama **Bring Me The Head of Mavis Davis** (1999), which starred Jane Horrocks, shot certain scenes.

Stanley Kubrick's **Eyes Wide Shut** (1999) filmed at a variety of locations around London, making particularly good use of Soho – especially Brewer Street and Eastcastle Street – which, like Holborn, stood in for parts of New York's Greenwich Village. The well-known Madame Jo-Jo's club on Brewer Street also doubled as the fictional New York jazz venue, Club Sonata.

Also set around Soho is Russell Mulcahy's spy thriller **Blue Ice** (1992). The film offered the intriguing notion of Michael Caine playing a former-British agent-but-now-jazz-club owner. It made use of the legendary Ronnie Scott's jazz club on Greek Street and featured a cherished cameo performance by the wonderful pianist-singer Bobby Short. The London *Blue Ice* presents is dark and seedy, but there is little substance to the movie.

Soho Square

Soho Square is rarely used in films, despite several film-associated companies, including 20th Century Fox and the British Board of Film Classification, having offices there. However, when it is seen, it provides an attractive backdrop, with its Tudor-style hut in the centre and a rare (for London) patch of grass that is much used as a lunch spot, cycle courier meeting point and venue for romantic assignations. Soho Square was used for a scene in the children's love story **Melody** (aka

A young Tommy Steele entertains customers of a Soho café in The Tommy Steele Story *(1957).*

S.W.A.L.K.) (1971, scripted by Alan Parker), and also in the restrained romantic drama **84 Charing Cross Road** (1987), which starred Anthony Hopkins and Anne Bancroft.

The children's film Melody *(aka* S.W.A.L.K.*) (1971) shot scenes in Soho.*

84 Charing Cross Road is based on Helene Hanff's autobiographical book about the relationship between a New Yorker (Bancroft) and Frank Doel (Hopkins), a mild-mannered manager of a bookshop (the 84 Charing Cross Road of the title). It is a relationship conducted entirely through letters that lasted for 29 years. When Bancroft's character finally does come to London to visit him, she finds the shop has closed and he has died. In one scene Doel is seen sitting outside Soho Square's pavilion, but despite the fact that the real 84 Charing Cross Road is actually just a few hundred yards from this location, most of the shooting took place at Shepperton Studios, to the south-west of London. Filming also took place in Richmond, which doubled for Frank Doel's home in Muswell Hill. In a cinematic twist, the character of Frank Doel was based on the father of screenwriter Leo Marks. He was the founder and owner of Marks & Co., the bookshop at 84 Charing Cross Road, though he never actually read Hanff's book. Leo Marks went on to write the screenplay for Michael Powell's London-set chiller *Peeping Tom* (1960) and was also the voice of Satan in Martin Scorsese's *The Last Temptation of Christ* (1988).

PICCADILLY

The UK's first cinema was opened on 21 March 1896 by cinematograph pioneer Birt Acres at 2 Piccadilly Mansions, located at the junction of Shaftesbury Avenue and Piccadilly Circus. Dubbed the Kineopticon, the venue showed a series of short silent films, but it was destroyed by fire shortly after opening.

The film-themed chain restaurant Planet Hollywood is also at this end of Piccadilly, located at 13 Coventry Street, next to the Trocadero shopping and

The Ritz hotel provides a glamorous backdrop to a variety of films.

amusement centre. The Planet Hollywood chain was set up by a group of movie mega-stars: Arnold Schwarzenegger, Sylvester Stallone, Bruce Willis and Demi Moore, with restaurateur Robert Earl. Set over three floors, the restaurant contains a large amount of framed movie memorabilia, naturally enough liberally scattered with items from the movie-star owners' films. Planet Hollywood was one of the many London locations used in **About a Boy** (2002).

The classic film noir **Night and the City** (1950), directed by Jules Dassin, showed London in a seedy and sinister light, with the director taking great pains to shoot at a number of notable sites around the city. The film stars Richard Widmark as Harry Fabian, an American hustler in London who thinks he can make it big with plans for Greco-Roman wrestling. The film shot at Piccadilly Circus and Trafalgar Square, with the fictional Silver Fox club located on St Martin's Lane. Filming also took place at St Paul's Cathedral, Westminster Bridge, the South Bank and Hammersmith.

The Ritz hotel on Piccadilly features regularly in movies. **In Notting Hill** (1999) it is perfectly used as the plush hotel where movie star Anna Scott (Julia Roberts) stays while promoting her latest film. When her potential lover William Thacker (Hugh Grant) comes to visit her, he is shown up to her suite of rooms as it is assumed he is part of the press junket that Scott is involved with. William pretends to be a journalist for *Horse and Hound* magazine with hilarious results. The Ritz also crops up in Neil Jordan's excellent crime film **Mona Lisa** (1986) in scenes where driver George (a remarkable performance by Bob Hoskins) takes prostitute Simone (Kathy Tyson) to the hotel for an 'appointment'. After an argument in the car he later stops the vehicle and dumps her out while circling nearby Hyde Park Corner.

The glamour of the hotel was exemplified in movies such as the romantic thriller **Dinner at the Ritz** (1937), starring David Niven and French actress Annabella (who later married American actor Tyrone Power) as a couple involved in a murder plot. Though mostly studio set, it highlighted the notion of the elegance and style of the hotel. In the camp spy thriller **Modesty Blaise** (1966) there is a scene of Modesty arriving for a meeting in the Ritz, being driven in an open-top blue Rolls Royce.

The nearby world-famous food emporium Fortnum & Mason was used for a scene in John Schlesinger's **Darling** (1965) in which ambitious actress Diana (an Oscar-winning performance by Julie Christie) engages in a little shoplifting with her friend Malcolm (Roland Curran). Fortnum & Mason can also be seen in **Howards End** (1992).

The elegant Burlington Arcade, on the opposite side of Piccadilly to The Ritz and Fortnum & Mason, can also be spotted frequently in films. It was one of the locations for the live-action adaptation of **101 Dalmatians** (1996), and was also used as the backdrop for a key scene in the thriller **Patriot Games** (1992), which starred Harrison Ford as CIA operative Jack Ryan. Early in *Patriot Games* a terrorist leaves a bookshop in Burlington Arcade and is followed by security operatives onto the tube (scenes that were shot at Aldwych station). The arcade can be seen in Brian Gilbert's drama **Tom & Viv** (1994), a story about poet T.S. Eliot (Willem Dafoe) and Vivienne Haigh-Wood (Miranda Richardson) the society girl he marries. Burlington Arcade also appears in the thriller **Incognito** (1997), directed by John Badham and starring Jason Patric and Irene Jacob.

Gangster No. 1 (2000) made use of the Park Lane Hotel on Piccadilly, while close to the hotel is Half Moon Street – a vital location in Bob Swaim's film of the same name. Based on Paul Theroux's novel *Dr Slaughter*, **Half Moon Street** (1986) starred Sigourney Weaver as an intelligent scholar by day and prostitute by night. The cast also included London stalwart Michael Caine. Michael Winner shot a scene nearby for his comedy caper **The Jokers** (1967) in a Jermyn Street club that would later become far better known as the celebrity hangout Tramp.

Piccadilly Circus

Piccadilly Circus and its environs can be seen in the cult hit **Croupier** (1999), directed by Mike Hodges. It stars Clive Owen as Jack Manfred, a croupier in a London casino who finds himself drawn into a plot to rob it. Much of the filming actually took place in a studio in Germany, but the distinctive central London scenes involving Manfred and Jani de Villiers (Alex Kingston) were shot in and around Piccadilly Circus.

Piccadilly Circus is one of those London sites that crops up regularly in the movies, but usually as a quick background image rather than as an

Clive Owen emerges from Piccadilly Circus tube station to the environs of casinos in the acclaimed drama Croupier (1999).

extensively used location. An honourable exception is the John Landis horror film **An American Werewolf in London** (1981), which shot its climax at Piccadilly Circus and the surrounding streets. Landis managed to persuade the authorities to shut down the area over two nights as he staged an ambitious series of scenes featuring a rampaging werewolf causing a spectacular multiple car pile-up.

The film is very much a tongue-in-cheek affair, starring David Naughton as Dave, and Griffin Dunne as Jack, two young American backpackers who are attacked by a werewolf in a misty field. Naughton finds himself transformed into a werewolf, but also manages to fall for a helpful London nurse (Jenny Agutter) who helps tend his wounds.

John Wayne visited Piccadilly Circus in **Brannigan** (1975); his investigations took him via most of London's key landmarks, and in Piccadilly Circus there is a mail-drop scene that sees the bad-guys

The statue of Eros at Piccadilly Circus was a companion for Peter Cook in the final scene of the 1967 version of Bedazzled.

escape via handily placed sewers. Piccadilly Circus can also be spotted – albeit briefly – in films as diverse as **The Day of the Triffids** (1962), Gurinder Chadha's comedy **Bend It Like Beckham** (2002) and **Bedazzled** (1967), in which Peter Cook as George Spiggot is seen standing next to the statue of Eros in the final scene.

PALL MALL

Jules Verne wrote his classic book *Around the World in Eighty Days* at the Reform Club, at 104 Pall Mall, and also wrote the club into the story by making it the starting (and finishing) point for his hero's journey around the world. The extravagant 1956 film **Around the World in Eighty Days** used exteriors of the club, as Phileas Fogg (David Niven) and his companion Passepartout (Cantiflas) set off to try and win a bet to travel around the world in 80 days. The club interiors were recreated at Elstree Studios in Hertfordshire. The film shot at various other London locations, including Hyde Park, Chelsea and Victoria.

In the James Bond film **Die Another Day** (2002), the exciting swordfight between Bond (Pierce Brosnan) and Gustav Graves (Toby Stephens) was shot in the Reform Club; the fencing scenes feature a cameo by Madonna as a fencing instructor. Meanwhile, in **The Avengers** (1998), Uma Thurman's Mrs Peel heads to the fictional Boodles Club for her first meeting with John Steed (Ralph Fiennes). The club – a place where supposedly there hasn't been a woman seen since 1762 – is actually the Reform Club, one of the more liberal of the species which does, in reality, have women members.

The nearby Royal Automobile Club on Pall Mall was used for scenes in Sally Potter's globe-trotting drama **The Man Who Cried** (2000), a film with a cast that included Johnny Depp, Christina Ricci and Cate Blanchett. Meanwhile, the Travellers' Club, also on Pall Mall, was used in scenes from Steve Norrington's **The Last Minute** (2000), starring Max Beesley and Emma Corrie, which also shot in Soho.

In **Bridget Jones's Diary** (2001), London's Institute for Contemporary Arts (ICA) in The Mall provided the background for a literary launch. The fictional party is attended by notable real-life literary figures such as Salman Rushdie, Julian Barnes, Sebastian Faulks and even Jeffrey Archer. Bridget (Renée Zellweger) makes a memorably awful – and unintentionally hilarious – speech, before being whisked off for a night of passion by her lusty boss Daniel Cleaver (Hugh Grant).

The Wings of the Dove (1991), an adaptation of the Henry James novel, locates the London home of Kate Croy (Helena Bonham Carter) – one of a pair of lovers who plot to swindle an American heiress – at 10 Carlton House Terrace, above The Mall; this is right next door to the administrative entrance to the ICA.

MAYFAIR

The final film starring The Beatles, **Let it Be** (1970), was made by director Michael Lindsay-Hogg as a documentary that showed the glorious realities of rehearsal, performance and studio recording. The film was made when the band was drifting apart, and there is a sense of tension to the whole production; many of The Beatles' associates had hoped that making the film would help the band stick together. Finished in 1969, the film – originally entitled *Get Back* – was not released until summer 1970. Filming took place at Twickenham Studios and at the Apple Studio. However, the most remarkable scene was the rooftop music session staged on top of the Apple Corporation's headquarters at 3 Savile Row, with John, Paul, George and Ringo performing a number of tracks, including 'Don't Let Me Down' and 'Get Back'. This was their last live performance.

Park Lane

Facing Hyde Park, Park Lane is an area of expensive hotels – including the Dorchester and The Metropolitan.

In **Dr No** (1962), James Bond – as played so effectively by Sean Connery – makes his first appearance at the *chemin-de-fer* table at Les Ambassadeurs, Hamilton Place, situated just behind the Hilton Hotel in Park Lane. Sadly, the scene was recreated in a studio, but Les Ambassadeurs was used for the scenes in **A Hard Day's Night** (1964) when the extremely un-Bondlike Wilfred Brambell (who plays Paul McCartney's grandfather in the film) sneaks off to indulge in a little gambling. The film also shot nightclub scenes at the club's Garrison Room.

The trendy Metropolitan Hotel (its Met Bar is a popular hangout for film folk and associated wannabes) was used in the romantic comedy **Notting Hill** (1999). In one scene the would-be lovers – played by Julia Roberts and Hugh Grant – have a meal at the hotel's pricey Nobu restaurant, only to overhear a group of fellow diners commenting nastily on the character played by Roberts, movie star Anna Scott.

Though most of the violent cult drama **Sexy Beast** (2000) was shot in Spain, certain key scenes were also shot in London. The film stars Ray Winstone as Gary

In Sexy Beast *(2000), Ian McShane (left) and Ray Winstone meet for a pre-heist breakfast in the Grosvener Hotel overlooking Hyde Park.*

Dove, a former gangster now happily retired to the Costa del Crime. However, he is forced out of retirement for a robbery by his gangster nemesis Don Logan (an Oscar-nominated performance by Ben Kingsley). When Gary (or Gal as he is known in the film) returns to London he stays at the Grosvenor Hotel on Upper Grosvenor Street. We see the character arriving at the hotel in a black cab, and before the robbery he has breakfast in the restaurant overlooking Park Lane.

Regent Street

North of Oxford Circus, on Regent Street, the Lumière brothers, Auguste and Louis, staged the first British presentation of their cinematograph. On 20 February 1896, in a special presentation to the press hosted by the magician Felicien Trewey, the brothers demonstrated their cinematic miracle at the Marlborough Hall, part of the London Polytechnic Institute at 309 Regent Street (it is now part of Westminster University). The following day the general public was allowed in.

Also on Regent Street, but south of Oxford Circus, is the world-famous toy shop Hamleys. The multi-level store was used as the location for the closing Christmas reconciliation scene between Tom Cruise and Nicole Kidman in the psychological drama **Eyes Wide Shut** (1999).

At the lower end of Regent Street, close to Piccadilly Circus, is the impressive Café Royal, which was used in a scene from James Ivory's **Maurice** (1987) when Clive Durham (Hugh Grant) dines with his family before leaving for mainland Europe.

Bond Street

South of Oxford Street and north of Piccadilly lies the exclusive shopping area of Bond Street and New Bond Street, much frequented by the rich and famous. In **Help!** (1965), directed by Richard Lester and starring The Beatles, drummer Ringo Starr finds himself with a ceremonial ring stuck on one of his fingers. This results in him being chased by a religious cult (headed by Eleanor Bron and Leo McKern) who want to retrieve the ring. The plot sees Ringo popping into jewellers Asprey's at 165 New Bond Street to try and have the offending trinket removed.

The exteriors of the auction house Sotheby's on Bond Street can be glimpsed in the James Bond film **Octopussy** (1983), directed by John Glen and starring Roger Moore as 007, in a scene where a Fabergé egg is put up for bidding; a studio stood in for the interiors of the famous auction house.

Selfridges

The well-known department store Selfridges has occasionally cropped up in movies. In Victor Saville's romantic comedy **Love on Wheels** (1932), which starred Jack Hulbert, filming had to wait until the evening when customers had made their way home. The store can also be seen in **Taxi for Two** (1929), which featured Mabel Poulton as a shop assistant in the hosiery department, and in the children's film **Just Ask for Diamond** (1988), directed by Stephen Bayly.

THE CITY & THE EAST END

The City of London is arguably the most important financial centre in the world and contains many of London's most dominant landmarks, many of which have appeared in numerous films over the years. The most effective use of one of the area's most major landmarks, Tower Bridge, was in **Brannigan** (1975), when John Wayne drove a car over the half-raised bridge.

More recently, film-makers have been keen to utilize the lesser-known parts of the City, such as Clerkenwell in **About a Boy** (2002), and traditional East End haunts, such as boys' boxing clubs and old-fashioned music halls.

The immediately recognizable dome of St Paul's Cathedral makes the location a favourite landmark for film directors.

BLACKFRIARS

On Her Majesty's Secret Service (1969) was the only James Bond film to feature Australian actor George Lazenby as everyone's favourite spy. In this episode Bond's mission is to go undercover in Switzerland in order to trap his arch-nemesis, Ernst Stavro Blofeld (Telly Savalas), who has ambitions to a grand (and rather bizarre) title – Monsieur le Comte Balthazar de Bleuville. Bond is required to disguise himself as a top official from the College of Arms and so he pays the institution, which is located on Queen Victoria Street in Blackfriars, a visit to research the role. The film's original script also included a scene in which Bond discovers one of Blofeld's men spying on his meeting with college bigwig Hilary Bray, whose identity Bond is to assume; the script also called for a chase sequence through the back streets and rooftops of London. However, Lazenby injured his arm while scaling a wall and the sequence was deleted from the final cut of the film.

Situated just north of Victoria Embankment, close to Blackfriars Bridge, are the Inns of Court, which were used for scenes in **A Fish Called Wanda** (1988). At nearby Middle Temple, the Grand Hall doubled as the elegant banqueting room in which Elizabeth I (Judi Dench) watches a performance of the play *Two Gentlemen of Verona* in a scene from the Oscar-winning **Shakespeare in Love** (1998).

FLEET STREET

Fleet Street was once the home of British newspapers, although now many are located in Docklands. When journalism was a popular movie theme the area was

often used by film-makers. In the classic British science-fiction film **The Day the Earth Caught Fire** (1961), directed by Val Guest, much of the filming took place at 121 Fleet Street in the wonderful Art Deco offices of *The Daily Express*.

Fleet Street provided the backdrop for The Day the Earth Caught Fire *(1961).*

THE CITY & THE EAST END

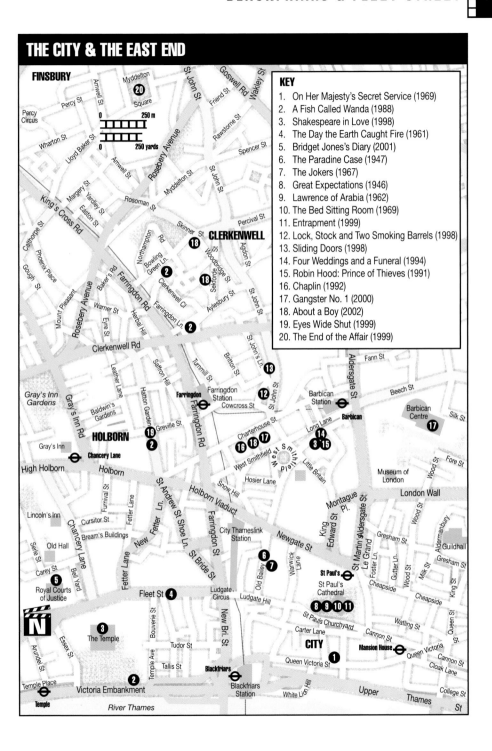

FINSBURY

CLERKENWELL

HOLBORN

CITY

KEY

1. On Her Majesty's Secret Service (1969)
2. A Fish Called Wanda (1988)
3. Shakespeare in Love (1998)
4. The Day the Earth Caught Fire (1961)
5. Bridget Jones's Diary (2001)
6. The Paradine Case (1947)
7. The Jokers (1967)
8. Great Expectations (1946)
9. Lawrence of Arabia (1962)
10. The Bed Sitting Room (1969)
11. Entrapment (1999)
12. Lock, Stock and Two Smoking Barrels (1998)
13. Sliding Doors (1998)
14. Four Weddings and a Funeral (1994)
15. Robin Hood: Prince of Thieves (1991)
16. Chaplin (1992)
17. Gangster No. 1 (2000)
18. About a Boy (2002)
19. Eyes Wide Shut (1999)
20. The End of the Affair (1999)

Close to Fleet Street are the Royal Courts of Justice, one of those institutions that regularly finds its way on to the big screen. In **Bridget Jones's Diary** (2001), Bridget, who has embarked on a new career as a cable television news presenter, runs to the shop across the road from the court to buy some cigarettes. Of course, in doing so, she misses her scoop, but luckily bumps into Mark Darcy (Colin Firth), who is the barrister of the man she is supposed to interview, and who saves the day.

OLD BAILEY

The exterior of the Central Criminal Court at the Old Bailey was used in Hitchcock's **The Paradine Case** (1947), although the interiors were shot in Hollywood. However, Michael Winner got permission to shoot inside the famed courthouse in his film **The Jokers** (1967), starring Oliver Reed and Sir Michael Crawford as a pair of brothers who steal the Crown jewels.

The scales of justice atop the Old Bailey featured in Michael Winner's The Jokers *(1967).*

ST PAUL'S CATHEDRAL

Christopher Wren's magnificent St Paul's Cathedral is much used in London-based films. In David Lean's wonderful adaptation of Charles Dickens' **Great Expectations** (1946), which starred John Mills, Alec Guinness, Bernard Miles and Jean Simmons, Lean shot the arrival of Pip (Mills) in front of the cathedral. Lean returned to the steps in front of St Paul's for one of the early scenes of his epic **Lawrence of Arabia** (1962), in which the crowds are seen leaving a memorial service for Lawrence. Somewhat poignantly, David Lean's own memorial service was held there in 1991.

The dome of St Paul's can be glimpsed in the comedy **The Bed Sitting Room** (1969). Based on the anti-war play by Spike Milligan and John Antrobus, the film is set three years after a nuclear war that has flooded London. The cathedral's roof can also be glimpsed in a scene in the caper thriller **Entrapment** (1999), starring Sean Connery and Catherine Zeta Jones, in a scene in which the duo head off to a Scottish castle via a helicopter trip that takes them over St Paul's.

SMITHFIELD

Vic Naylor's bar at 40 St John Street, close to Smithfield meat market, was the location for the bar run by J.D. (Sting) in **Lock, Stock and Two Smoking Barrels** (1998). Also on St John Street is the apartment where Lydia (Jeanne Tripplehorn) lives in the romantic comedy **Sliding Doors** (1998), which also stars Gwyneth Paltrow as Helen. In the film, Lydia lives at Pattern House, St John Street, and it is to here that Helen follows her boyfriend, Gerry (Jon Lynch), and confronts him in a tryst with Lydia.

In **Four Weddings and a Funeral** (1994), wedding number four is set in the church of St Bartholomew the Great in Smithfield. The wedding sees Charles (Hugh Grant) set to marry Henrietta aka Duck Face (Anna Chancellor). However, he has second thoughts when he realizes that he really loves Carrie (Andie MacDowell). The same church doubled as the interior of Nottingham Cathedral for **Robin Hood: Prince of Thieves** (1991), in a scene in which Kevin Costner's Robin has to rescue his Maid Marian (Mary Elizabeth Mastrantonio) from the evil clutches of the Sheriff (a wonderfully over-the-top performance from Alan Rickman). The church also served as a location in **Shakespeare in Love** (1998), in a scene in which Shakespeare (Joseph Fiennes) visits the church to beg God's forgiveness after the murder of fellow playwright Christopher Marlowe (a telling cameo from Rupert Everett).

Smithfield also provides the backdrop for some scenes from Richard Attenborough's biopic **Chaplin** (1992), which starred Robert Downey Jr as the famous comedian. In the film, we see Chaplin taking his first love Hetty Kelly (Moira Kelly) for a cup of tea at the old Covent Garden flower market. The famous old Smithfield meat market doubled as Covent Garden market, which has moved south of the river to new premises at Nine Elms.

BARBICAN

A complex of high- and low-rise apartments, theatres and concert halls, the Barbican centre has been the subject of much controversy since it was constructed in the 1960s. However, love it or hate it, it's now very much a part of London's landscape and an intriguing location for film-makers.

The tough London-set crime film **Gangster No 1** (2000), directed by Paul McGuigan – who made the FilmFour *Acid House Trilogy* – is told partly as a voiceover by Malcolm McDowell as Gangster No. 1 tracing the different events during his life. Young Gangster No. 1 is played by Paul Bettany, who went on to appear alongside Russell Crowe in *A Beautiful Mind* (2001), while Saffron Burrows plays Karen, the woman who comes between Gangster and his boss.

The 'sixties architecture of the Barbican complex makes it a great period location.

'**W**e chose everything that was 'sixties modern, such as [the character] Freddie Mays's flat in the Barbican, which is one of the big images in the film.'

RICHARD BRIDGLAND,
PRODUCTION DESIGNER,
GANGSTER NO.1

Production designer Richard Bridgland was charged with reinventing the look of London *circa* 1968, and to do so referred to photographs from the era, particularly those of Erwin Fieger.

The team chose to avoid the 'grey-terraced streets' look they felt had characterized many previous movies on London's gangland. 'Terraced streets shrink a movie to the size of a domestic drama,' said Bridgland. 'Because the story comes from Gangster's perspective, it creates a fascinating psychological space. That, and the script's mythic quality, makes you want to open it out.'

In addition to shooting at the Barbican, locations were found at many other atmospheric London locations, including the nearby Cock Tavern in Smithfield Market, King's Cross, the Old Kent Road, Russell Square, the Park Lane Hotel in Piccadilly, the Café de Paris in Leicester Square and Trinity Buoy Wharf, opposite the Millennium Dome.

CLERKENWELL

The hit comedy **About a Boy** (2002), directed by Chris and Paul Weitz and based on Nick Hornby's successful novel of the same name, was shot at a number of London locations, though largely based around Clerkenwell, an area north of the City that has been revitalized in recent decades. Cast and crew spent seven weeks in the area creating the world of Will, expertly played by Hugh Grant. Co-producer Nicky Kentish-Barnes commented: 'Clerkenwell hasn't been used much as a London film location so we are contributing something new.' Production designer Jim Clay added: 'This is a different London, a real London. London is a vibrant and fabulous place to live and that was the world we wanted to put into the movie, rather than the traditionally perceived world of old London town.'

The character of Will is a carefree – and careless – single man who discovers a good way to meet women and avoid commitment is to try and date women who are single parents. However, his plans begin to unravel when he cons his way into a support group for single parents. There he meets lonely 12-year-old, Marcus (Nicholas Hoult), who is to have a profound influence on him. The film then traces the relationship between the two, as Marcus, avoiding his fragile domestic situation (his mother suffers from chronic depression), adopts Will as his friend.

> **'This is a different London, a real London. London is a vibrant and fabulous place to live…'**
>
> JIM CLAY, PRODUCTION DESIGNER, *ABOUT A BOY*

The area is well used in the film. The venue where the single-parents' group SPAT hold their meetings is in the basement of the Clerkenwell and Islington Medical Mission, Woodbridge Chapel, Woodbridge Street. The exterior of Will's ultra-trendy apartment is actually the old 'Help the Aged' building at the junction of Sekforde Street and St James Walk on Clerkenwell, while the deli he visits in one scene is actually Compton Gascon, Charterhouse Street.

Other London locations for *About a Boy* included a supermarket in Richmond, Planet Hollywood, the IMAX cinema at Waterloo and Regent's Park.

Between Holborn and Clerkenwell is the famous jewellers' street, Hatton Garden. It doubled as New York's Greenwich Village in Stanley Kubrick's final film **Eyes Wide Shut** (1999), and was used for the initial robbery scenes in the comedy **A Fish Called Wanda** (1988) starring Jamie Lee Curtis, John Cleese, Michael Palin

LOCATION LONDON

FILM PIONEER *Robert William Paul*

DATES *1869-1943*

Film pioneer **Robert William Paul** had his workshop at 44 Hatton Garden. Born at 3 Albion Place, off Liverpool Road, Highbury, he worked as an instrument maker and electrical engineer, and in 1894 was approached by two Greek entrepreneurs to make copies of Thomas Edison's peepshow device Kinetoscope, which hadn't been patented in the UK. He later joined up with photographer Birt Acres and they built the UK's first moving picture camera before making a series of short films, including *The Arrest of a Pickpocket* and *The Derby*, which are among the UK's earliest films.

and Kevin Kline. In the film we see the character Wanda, played by Jamie Lee Curtis, surveying the Diamond House at 37–38 Hatton Garden. After staging a diamond robbery in Hatton Garden, the criminal gang make their getaway via Clerkenwell. Jamie Lee Curtis (dressed as a man, replete with false moustache) waits in a car in Clerkenwell Green, while the set of steps where the gang exchange escape cars is between Clerkenwell Close and Robert's Place.

Just south of the Pentonville Road, on the edge of Clerkenwell, is Myddleton Square, where scenes from Neil Jordan's wartime drama **The End of the Affair** (1999), based on Graham Greene's novel of the same name, were shot.

THE FINANCIAL CENTRE

Although the majority of Taylor Hackford's **Proof of Life** (2001) was shot in Ecuador, with some scenes filmed in Poland, London is where we first meet the main character, Terry Thorne (Russell Crowe). Thorne works for an insurance company that specializes in kidnap and ransom situations. The plot takes the character to Latin America where he negotiates the rescue of a kidnapped American construction worker, played by David Morse. There is a hint of romance as Thorne becomes

The Lloyd's of London building featured in Proof of Life *(2001), which starred Russell Crowe and Meg Ryan.*

'**W**e were able to use one of the most beautiful and modern buildings in all of Europe, Lloyd's Of London, which is a spectacular, ultra-modern, ultra-commercial building. It reeks of capitalism.'

TAYLOR HACKFORD, DIRECTOR, *PROOF OF LIFE*

THE CITY & THE EAST END

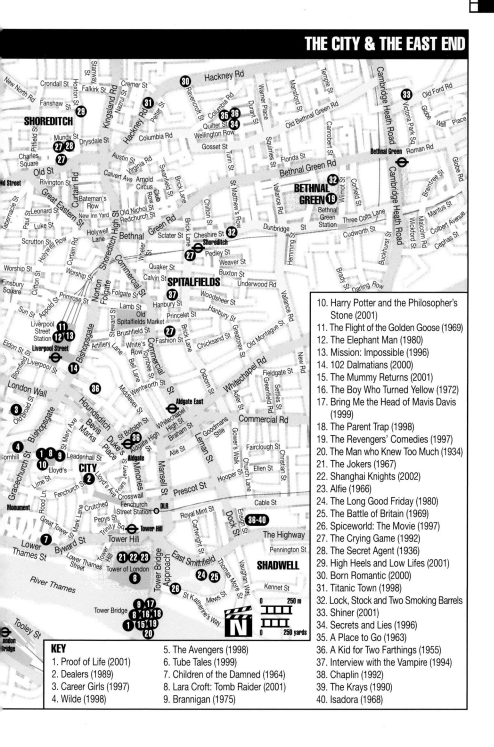

10. Harry Potter and the Philosopher's Stone (2001)
11. The Flight of the Golden Goose (1969)
12. The Elephant Man (1980)
13. Mission: Impossible (1996)
14. 102 Dalmatians (2000)
15. The Mummy Returns (2001)
16. The Boy Who Turned Yellow (1972)
17. Bring Me the Head of Mavis Davis (1999)
18. The Parent Trap (1998)
19. The Revengers' Comedies (1997)
20. The Man who Knew Too Much (1934)
21. The Jokers (1967)
22. Shanghai Knights (2002)
23. Alfie (1966)
24. The Long Good Friday (1980)
25. The Battle of Britain (1969)
26. Spiceworld: The Movie (1997)
27. The Crying Game (1992)
28. The Secret Agent (1936)
29. High Heels and Low Lifes (2001)
30. Born Romantic (2000)
31. Titanic Town (1998)
32. Lock, Stock and Two Smoking Barrels
33. Shiner (2001)
34. Secrets and Lies (1996)
35. A Place to Go (1963)
36. A Kid for Two Farthings (1955)
37. Interview with the Vampire (1994)
38. Chaplin (1992)
39. The Krays (1990)
40. Isadora (1968)

KEY

1. Proof of Life (2001)
2. Dealers (1989)
3. Career Girls (1997)
4. Wilde (1998)
5. The Avengers (1998)
6. Tube Tales (1999)
7. Children of the Damned (1964)
8. Lara Croft: Tomb Raider (2001)
9. Brannigan (1975)

Paul McGann and Rebecca de Mornay in the City film Dealers *(1989).*

close to the hostage's wife, Alice, who is played by Meg Ryan. Scenes of the company headquarters were shot in the City, and as Taylor Hackford explained: 'We were able to use one of the most beautiful and modern buildings in all of Europe, Lloyd's Of London, which is a spectacular, ultra-modern, ultra-commercial building. It reeks of capitalism.' The Lloyd's Building is the work of acclaimed British architect Lord Richard Rogers; early in the film Crowe leaves a meeting via one of the building's sensational glass lifts, which offers spectacular views of St Paul's Cathedral and the City.

The production was also able to shoot at a café called The Saigon Times in Leadenhall Market, and on a luxury yacht, *The Silver Sturgeon*, on the River Thames against the backdrop of Tower Bridge. The interior London scenes were shot at Pinewood Studios, home to many of the James Bond films.

The City also plays a key role in a rather limp British attempt to build on the success of Oliver Stone's financial drama *Wall Street* (1987). Paul McGann and Rebecca De Mornay headed the cast in **Dealers** (1989), a drama about the lives of wealthy young traders in the City; unfortunately, the film came out just as the UK's financial bubble burst. One of the City's major financial institutions can be spotted in Mike Leigh's **Career Girls** (1997) – the two key characters, Hannah (Katrin Cartlidge) and Annie (Lynda Steadman), are shown around a fashionable Docklands apartment with views of the NatWest Tower.

In the heart of the city is the historic Jamaica Wine Lodge, which can be found at St Michael's Alley, Cornhill. It featured in a scene from Brian Gilbert's biopic **Wilde** (1998) in which Robert Ross (Michael Sheen) consoles one of the title character's former lovers, John Gray, played by a young Ioan Gruffudd.

Meanwhile, Bank tube station, in the heart of the financial centre, appeared in the big-budget big-screen version of **The Avengers** (1998), starring Ralph Fiennes and Uma Thurman. The station also had what could be seen as the lead role in **Tube Tales** (1999), a film that comprised a series of short movies, the plots of which centered on the London Underground; the cast included Rachel Weisz and Ray Winstone.

The lovely City church of St Dunstan-in-the-East, St Dunstan's Hill featured in the British chiller **Children of the Damned** (1964). A sequel to *Village of the Damned* (1960) – itself an adaptation of John Wyndham's book *The Midwich Cuckoos* – it continued the story of strange mutated blond children with plans for world domination. The church was used for the closing scenes as the youngsters shelter in the building.

Leadenhall Market

In **Lara Croft: Tomb Raider** (2001), Lara – played with gusto by Angelina Jolie – can be seen speeding over Tower Bridge on her powerful black motorcycle on her way to an important auction and a meeting with Wilson (Leslie Phillips), an old friend of her late father. As she leaves that meeting, Lara heads through nearby Leadenhall Market. The film, directed by Simon West, also includes the obligatory glimpse of the Tower of London as Lara speeds – this time in a car – through the London streets for an assignation with the bad guy, Manfred Powell (Iain Glen).

Leadenhall Market was also used for a key scene in **Brannigan (1975)**. No John Wayne film would be complete without the bar-room punch-up that characterized most of his Westerns, and in this movie it took place at Leadenhall's Lamb Tavern. Leadenhall Market can also be seen in the international blockbuster **Harry Potter and the Philosopher's Stone** (US title: **Harry Potter and the Sorcerer's Stone** 2001) where it was transformed into Diagon Alley, the place where wizards go to shop.

John Wayne once got into a bar-room brawl in the Lamb Tavern. Fortunately it was part of his role in the 1970s film Brannigan.

John Hurt in Liverpool Street Station in his award-winning role as John Merrick in The Elephant Man *(1980).*

Liverpool Street Station

This vast terminus on the edge of the City has also been used as a cinematic backdrop in several films. It featured in **The Flight of the Golden Goose** (1969), starring Yul Brynner, and in David Lynch's black-and-white masterpiece, **The Elephant Man** (1980). Set in the late 19th century we see John Hurt, who plays the deformed title character John Merrick, arriving at a Victorian London railway station after leaving the freak show. Liverpool Street was perfect for the scene when Lynch shot there in the late 'seventies, but it has since been redeveloped and couldn't feature as a period location any more.

Since then, though, the station has been used for scenes in **Mission: Impossible** (1996), directed by Brian De Palma and starring Tom Cruise as secret agent Ethan Hunt. Having been set up in Prague, Ethan and his team of agents are on the run in London, and hole-up in a safe-house on Broad Street, above Liverpool Street tube station. Ethan heads off to telephone boxes at the railway station where he meets his boss, who is played by Jon Voight.

Bishopsgate

Much of **102 Dalmatians** (2000) was shot in studios, though there are many exterior London shots. The set for Le Pelt's fur fashion show was actually built at an old tram depot in Bishopsgate in London. 'It was dirty and dank and made a terrific backdrop for Le Pelt's show.' said the film's production designer Assheton Gordon.

TOWER BRIDGE

Naturally enough, Tower Bridge is one of those London landmarks that often crops up in movies, though more often than not as an establishing shot – to confirm to viewers that, yes, we actually are in London, England – rather than as a fully-fledged filming location.

One film which did make proper use of Tower Bridge – in rather typical Hollywood stunt fashion – was the John Wayne action film **Brannigan** (1975), the one and only film 'the Duke' made in Britain. The film offered the humorous little-and-large pairing of John Wayne and Richard Attenborough (as a Scotland Yard detective),

Tower Bridge was used to full effect by director Douglas Hickox in the John Wayne film Brannigan *(1975).*

and a cast also featuring Judy Geeson, Mel Ferrer and Lesley-Anne Down. Wayne played a tough Chicago cop chasing a bad guy from his home city. The legendary star took the film as a reaction to seeing Clint Eastwood's cop movie *Coogan's Bluff* (1968), a script that he was offered and regretted not taking on viewing the final movie. Directed by British director Douglas Hickox, *Brannigan* was shot around London using pretty much every well-known landmark, including staging a spectacular car jump over the half-opened Tower Bridge.

Tower Bridge also provided a wonderful setting for one of the major action scenes in **The Mummy Returns** (2001). The pivotal London chase scene involves Rick (Brendan Fraser) and Evie (Rachel Weisz), along with their son Alex (Freddie Boath), her brother Jonathan (John Hannah) and friend Ardeth Bey (Oded Fehr), being pursued by four rampaging mummies across London from the British Museum to Tower Bridge. The action took place on vintage red London buses, which were rounded up from private collections from as far away as Wales and Belgium, restored and dressed for the shoot, and adorned with real advertisements from the era, yet in the film it is made to seem as though just one bus was used.

Sean Daniel, a producer of *The Mummy Returns* said they had originally envisioned an entirely London-based shoot, but the film's story expanded to feature the Moroccan desert. Once back in London, the cast and crew quickly became nostalgic for the Moroccan sun as the city's weather was appalling. 'Everyone told me that it was the worst British summer in years,' added another of the film's producers, James Jacks, 'It was rainy and chilly and our night shooting was constantly interrupted by weather and rainstorms.'

Tower Bridge also appeared in several other films, including **The Boy Who Turned Yellow** (1972), directed by Michael Powell; **Bring Me The Head of Mavis Davis** (1999), which starred Jane Horrocks and Rik Mayall; **The Parent Trap** (1998), starring Dennis Quaid and Natasha Richardson and **The Revengers' Comedies** (1997), which featured Helena Bonham Carter and Sam Neill. The distinctive bridge

The Tower of London features in two films from the 1960s: Alfie *(1966) and* The Jokers *(1967).*

can also be spotted briefly in Hitchcock's first version of **The Man Who Knew Too Much** (1934) – in those days the nearby docks were still working sites.

Tower of London

Director Michael Winner used his not-inconsiderable powers of persuasion to get permission to film his comedy-caper **The Jokers** (1967) at the Tower of London. The fact that the film is actually about two brothers – played by Michael Crawford and Oliver Reed – who actually manage to steal the crown jewels makes this even more impressive. Not only do they manage to get away with their cunning – and very amusing – plan, but they then return the jewels by placing them in the Scales of Justice on the top of the Old Bailey.

    Shanghai Knights (2002), directed by David Dobkin, was the sequel to the successful comedy-action Western *Shanghai Noon* (2000) and also makes use of the Tower of London. The film stars Jackie Chan and Owen Wilson as a mis-matched duo who travel back in time to Victorian London to foil an evil plot. The script called for filming at the Tower of London and in a wax museum.

    The historic fortress can also be seen in Lewis Gilbert's **Alfie** (1966), starring Michael Caine in the title role. Womanizing Alfie does some work as a street photographer, a job that takes him to places such as the Houses of Parliament and the Tower of London, where he meets up with girlfriend Ruby (Shelley Winters).

St Katherine's Dock

Close to Tower Bridge, on the north side of the Thames, is St Katherine's Dock, which provided the backdrop for a number of key scenes from John Mackenzie's tough gangster film **The Long Good Friday** (1980). The film starred Bob Hoskins, in one of his first big-screen roles, as mobster Harold Shand, with Helen Mirren as his sophisticated girlfriend Victoria. St Katherine's Dock also features in the epic war film **The Battle of Britain** (1969), which had a stellar cast that included Laurence Olivier, Robert Shaw and Christopher Plummer. Sections of the dock's warehouses were set alight by a special-effects team to imitate scenes of London devastated by Nazi bombing.

Next to the docks, in St Katherine's Way, is the Tower Hotel, which was used in Bob Spiers' film starring the British girl group the Spice Girls, **Spiceworld: The Movie** (1997). The hotel's café featured in the film, though the film also made use of many other London locations as the girls were driven around in a double-decker bus.

HOXTON, SHOREDITCH & SPITALFIELDS

Once rundown, forgotten areas of east London, the now trendy areas of Hoxton, Shoreditch and Spitalfields play home to artists, clubbers – and film crews.

The area was used as a location for Neil Jordan's acclaimed drama **The Crying Game** (1992). Stephen Rea played Fergus, an IRA man who becomes involved with Dil, the London-based partner of a soldier he was supposed to kill in Ulster. The Spitalfields hairdresser in which Dil (Jaye Davidson) works was actually an empty factory at 3 Fournier Street, while the fictional Metro Bar where Dil sings the title song was shot at 333 (a gay bar at the time of filming) at 333 Old Street. The exterior of the club, though, is actually a building at nearby 28–30 Coronet Street, just off Hoxton Square, which was dressed as a bar. Dil's flat was located at 9 Hoxton Square, while the square provided the backdrop for the scene in which Fergus gazes at Dil standing in some gardens. *The Crying Game* also shot scenes at Brick Lane, a little further east, and at several other London locations.

Long before Hoxton Square became fashionable, Alfred Hitchcock made use of it when shooting elements of his spy thriller **The Secret Agent** (1936). The film featured John Gielgud as the heroic spy Richard Ashenden, with the rest of a wonderful cast including Peter Lorre, Madeleine Carroll and Robert Young.

As well as shooting in Hackney, Mel Smith's **High Heels and Low Lifes** (2001), made use of Hoxton. In the film, Shannon (Minnie Driver) and Frances (Mary McCormack) stumble across a robbery and start – as a black joke – to blackmail the robbers, but then matters soon start getting nasty and they find themselves being pursued around London by the armed mobsters.

'I believe we've achieved a real "Greenwich Village, New York" feel in that we found interesting, urban, chic settings with a great heart to where the girls live, work and socialize – a real community.'

SARAH LEE, LOCATION MANAGER,
HIGH HEELS AND LOW LIFES

Although much of the film was shot at Ealing Studios, several scenes were filmed in the hip areas of Hoxton, Hackney and Hatton Garden. The girls' dynamic urban lifestyles contrast with picturesque rural settings in Surrey and Kent where the robbers live. Location manager Sarah Lee explained her reason for choosing Hoxton. 'We were trying to give the film a style that hasn't been seen before in contemporary British cinema', and director Mel Smith added: 'We've shot London in a way you don't normally see. There's a great sense of scale – there's a lot of really spectacular aerial photography. It makes London very sexy, I think.'

Born Romantic (2000), the second film from David Kane (his first was the romantic drama *This Year's Love*, which was shot in London's Camden Town), is very much a London film, and follows three men and three women as they struggle to find love in the city. The trio of couples – played by, among others, Jane Horrocks, Jimi Mistry and Olivia Williams – are connected by two key things. First, they all take taxis around the city and receive advice from the cab driver Jimmy (Adrian Lester), and secondly they all like to meet and dance at a local Salsa club. The film also shot on locations in north and east London around Hoxton, Clerkenwell, Shoreditch and Hackney.

Hackney Road, just off Shoreditch, was transformed into the Belfast of 1972 for a scene in the powerful drama **Titanic Town** (1998), based on the semi-autobiographical novel by Mary Costello. Julie Walters plays Bernie McPhelimy, a Catholic housewife who tries to bring peace to the region.

BETHNAL GREEN

The heart of the East End of London to many, Bethnal Green is synonymous with a certain 1960s feel – notorious for its links with the criminal underworld of that period, particularly the antics of the Kray Twins. Perhaps not surprisingly, this thriving area is a popular location for crime films to shoot.

The British crime film **Lock, Stock and Two Smoking Barrels** (1998), directed by Guy Ritchie, shot the scenes set in a seedy office of a supposed Soho sex club at Bethnal Green Town Hall, a building that also appears in **The Revengers' Comedies** (1997). The boxing scenes in *Lock, Stock …* were set at Repton Boys Club and at a club on St John Street near Smithfield Market.

Another crime film to use Bethnal Green as a backdrop was **Shiner** (2001), in which Michael Caine plays Billy 'Shiner' Simpson, a small-time boxing promoter with big ideas. His son competes in a title fight with an American champion, but when he loses and is subsequently shot, Billy sets about trying to uncover the killer and a possible conspiracy.

The film used Bethnal Green's York Hall as the venue for the film's boxing match, which is appropriate as it is a genuine East End fight arena. Director John Irvin said: 'Throughout the film I wanted to see the genuine article. I was shown York Hall on the first day of researching the story. It was perfect! I couldn't believe it – day one and I had found my principal location.'

In Mike Leigh's **Secrets and Lies** (1996) the terraced house in which Cynthia (played with gusto by Brenda Blethyn) lives is actually 76 Quilter Street, Bethnal Green. This part of the East End also provided a location for the drama **A Place to Go** (1963), starring Rita Tushingham and Bernard Lee, and **A Kid For Two Farthings** (1955), starring Diana Dors and David Kossoff.

WHITECHAPEL

Interview with the Vampire (1994), Neil Jordan's stylish period adaptation of Anne Rice's bestseller, created much controversy at the time with the casting of Tom Cruise as the charismatic vampire Lestat de Lioncourt, as Rice didn't think Cruise was right for the part. Rice subsequently made a very public change of mind after seeing the film. Shooting largely took place in San Francisco and Louisiana, though certain scenes were shot at St Paul's Church, Deptford, Spitalfields and in Wilton's Music Hall at Grace's Alley, Ensign Street in Whitechapel.

The historic Wilton's Music Hall is also used in a pivotal scene – supposedly set in Aldershot – in **Chaplin** (1992), in which a young Charlie helps his mother's floundering stage act. Wilton's Music Hall has featured in other movies, such as **The Krays** (1990) and **Isadora** (1968). In Carol Reed's sentimental drama **A Kid for Two Farthings** (1955), nearby Petticoat Lane doubles as 'Fashion Street', while Aldgate can also be seen in the film.

Charlie Chaplin (1889–1977) was one of the greatest stars of the silent comedy. The biographical film Chaplin *(1992) filmed in Whitechapel.*

NORTH-WEST LONDON

Wealthy and attractive areas such as Hampstead and Highgate can regularly be spotted in films. Kenwood House, the beautiful stately home sitting at the top of Hampstead Heath, saw a substantial rise in visitor numbers after it featured in the romantic comedy **Notting Hill** (1999). North-west London is a very rich and diverse urban area, with film-makers quick to appreciate the variety of backdrops offered by areas such as Camden, Regent's Park, the Gothic St Pancras Station and the evocative cemetery at Kensal Green. Film-makers have even seen the potential of the multi-storey car-park at the Brent Cross Shopping Centre – where James Bond engaged in a little motor mayhem by remote control in **Tomorrow Never Dies** (1997).

The vibrancy of Camden Lock on Regent's Canal has suited several UK-made romantic comedies, including *This Year's Love* (1999) and *Jack & Sarah* (1995).

KING'S CROSS & ST PANCRAS

King's Cross

Cheney Road, a winding cobbled street situated behind King's Cross station is a favourite spot for film-makers, especially when it comes to recreating the East End of years gone by. Some of the many films that have shot there include **The Missionary** (1983), **Shirley Valentine** (1989), **Nuns on the Run** (1990), **The Secret Garden** (1993) and **Richard III** (1995). The street also doubled for 1960s Liverpool for the drama **Backbeat** (1993), directed by Iain Softley, which re-told the early years of The Beatles. The opening Liverpool-set scene sees Stuart Sutcliffe (Stephen Dorff) getting involved in a fight with John Lennon and Cheney Road stood in for the northern city.

One of the most famous British movies to make great use of the area, including Cheney Road, is the Ealing black comedy **The Ladykillers** (1955). Directed by Sandy Mackendrick, it starred Alec Guinness – wearing hilarious pantomime teeth in a role originally to be played by Alastair Sim – as the leader of a band of crooks played by Peter Sellers, Herbert Lom, Cecil Parker and Danny Green. The criminals rent rooms in the house of sweet old Mrs Wilberforce (Katie Johnson), claiming to be using the accommodation to practise music, when they are actually plotting a robbery. Mrs Wilberforce's house was built by the producers at the end of Frederica Street, just off the Caledonian Road, an area that has since been redeveloped.

Alec Guinness (left) helps dispose of yet another body onto the railway tracks at King's Cross in the classic comedy The Ladykillers *(1955).*

NORTH-WEST LONDON

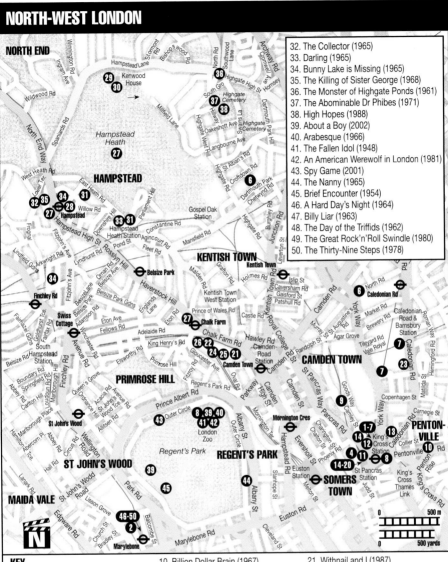

NORTH END

Kenwood House

Hampstead Heath

HAMPSTEAD

Hampstead Heath

KENTISH TOWN

Belsize Park

Finchley Rd

Swiss Cottage

Chalk Farm

PRIMROSE HILL

Camden Town

CAMDEN TOWN

St John's Wood

London Zoo

PENTON-VILLE

REGENT'S PARK

ST JOHN'S WOOD

SOMERS TOWN

MAIDA VALE

32. The Collector (1965)
33. Darling (1965)
34. Bunny Lake is Missing (1965)
35. The Killing of Sister George (1968)
36. The Monster of Highgate Ponds (1961)
37. The Abominable Dr Phibes (1971)
38. High Hopes (1988)
39. About a Boy (2002)
40. Arabesque (1966)
41. The Fallen Idol (1948)
42. An American Werewolf in London (1981)
43. Spy Game (2001)
44. The Nanny (1965)
45. Brief Encounter (1954)
46. A Hard Day's Night (1964)
47. Billy Liar (1963)
48. The Day of the Triffids (1962)
49. The Great Rock'n'Roll Swindle (1980)
50. The Thirty-Nine Steps (1978)

0   500 m

0   500 yards

KEY

1. Missionary (1983)
2. Shirley Valentine (1989)
3. Nuns on the Run (1990)
4. The Secret Garden (1993)
5. Richard III (1995)
6. Backbeat (1993)
7. The Ladykillers (1955)
8. Harry Potter and the Philosopher's Stone (2001)
9. Alfie (1966)
10. Billion Dollar Brain (1967)
11. High Hopes (1988)
12. Career Girls (1997)
13. Mona Lisa (1986)
14. Chaplin (1992)
15. Spider (2002)
16. Howards End (1992)
17. 102 Dalmatians (2000)
18. Batman (1989)
19. Shining Through (1992)
20. Bridget Jones's Diary (2001)
21. Withnail and I (1987)
22. This Year's Love (1999)
23. The Tall Guy (1989)
24. Jack and Sarah (1995)
25. The Music Lovers (1970)
26. Death Machine (1994)
27. The Boy Who Turned Yellow (1972)
28. Wanted for Murder (1946)
29. 101 Dalmatians (1996)
30. Notting Hill (1999)
31. Dance with a Stranger (1985)

The magnificent Gothic facade of St Pancras has featured in several fantasy films, including Batman *(1989) and* Harry Potter and the Philosopher's Stone *(2001).*

After the robbery has been pulled off, the gang returns to the house with their loot, after which they start bickering. Mrs Wilberforce discovers the plot to kill her off, but before she can be dispatched, the crooks, undecided as to who will do the killing, actually begin to kill each other. As the bodies start to fall, they are dumped at the nearby Copenhagen Tunnel. A replica of the tunnel was built at Ealing Studios for the close-up scenes, but great use is made of the actual railway tracks and tunnels. When shooting wrapped, the producers thanked the residents of Frederica Street for the disruption caused by the filming by staging a street party hosted by cast and crew.

King's Cross Station also played a vital role in **Harry Potter and the Philosopher's Stone** (US title: **Harry Potter and the Sorcerer's Stone,** 2001). Platform Four doubled as the fictional Platform Nine and Three-quarters, where young Harry has to join his schoolmates to board the Hogwarts' Express. In the follow-up film, **Harry Potter and the Chamber of Secrets** (2002), it is the gothic exterior of St Pancras Station that is used.

After the opening credits of the drama **Alfie** (1966), which were shot on Vauxhall Bridge, the film swiftly moves to Camley Street, just behind King's Cross Station, where Alfie (Michael Caine) is seen engaging in a little car-bound loving with Siddie (Millicent Martin). As the film draws on, he romances a series of women around the capital. Michael Caine can also be spotted in the King's Cross area in **Billion Dollar Brain** (1967), the third of his Harry Palmer films, which was directed by Ken Russell. The seedy apartment where Caine's blue-collar spy Harry Palmer lives is actually at 297 Pentonville Road, opposite King's Cross Station.

Mike Leigh shot scenes from his film **High Hopes** (1988) just behind King's Cross. The flat in which Cyril (Philip Davis) and Shirley (Ruth Sheen) live is on Stanley

Passage, which runs between Cheney Road and Pancras Road. Mike Leigh returned to the area for an early scene in **Career Girls** (1997), which sees Annie (Lynda Steadman) arriving at King's Cross to meet up with her old college friend Hannah (Katrin Cartlidge). The gritty back streets behind the station were also used in a scene from the crime drama **Mona Lisa** (1986), when George (Bob Hoskins) is searching for a prostitute friend of Simone (Kathy Tyson).

St Pancras

In Richard Attenborough's biopic **Chaplin** (1992), Cheney Road and nearby Battle Bridge Road were used to double as Lambeth for scenes of the comedian's early life. Further west along the Euston Road is the Gothic old St Pancras Hotel, which sits impressively above – and as a frontage to – St Pancras Station, and which doubled as the asylum where Chaplin's mother is placed. St Pancras Station itself was also used as a double for Waterloo Station in the scenes of Chaplin's return to London from Hollywood. David Cronenberg's disturbing drama **Spider** (2002), starring Ralph Fiennes and Miranda Richardson, saw St Pancras standing in for Waterloo again in the film's opening scene.

The ticket hall at St Pancras is used in **Howards End** (1992) for a scene in which Margaret Schlegel (Emma Thompson) buys a ticket to take her to the fictional village of Hilton, where the house that gives the film its title is located. The station can also be seen in Kevin Lima's **102 Dalmatians** (2000) as the cuddly pups head off to France (although in reality trains from the station head north of London). St Pancras Chambers (part of the old St Pancras Hotel) was used as a location for Tim Burton's **Batman** (1989), which starred Michael Keaton as the caped crusader. The Chambers also featured in an engaging version of the classic children's novel **The Secret Garden** (1993). Much of the film was shot in Yorkshire, although St Pancras Chambers provided the staircase inside Mistlethwaite Manor, the gloomy home where Mary Lennox (Kate Maberly) goes to live after the death of her parents, and where she discovers the secret garden of the title. In the war romance **Shining**

LOCATION LONDON

ACTOR *Kenneth Williams*

DATES *1926-1988*

The classically camp comedian **Kenneth Williams** was born at Bingfield Street, just off the Caledonian Road, on February 22, 1926, though a few years later his family moved to the flat above the hairdresser shop run by his father Charlie Williams at 57 Marchmont Street. Initially a star on radio shows such as *Hancock's Half Hour* and *Round the Horne*, real fame came with Williams's regular appearances in the series of *Carry On* film comedies.

Through (1992), which starred Michael Douglas and Melanie Griffith, St Pancras stood in for the Swiss city of Zürich, with other scenes shot at Aldwych and Greenwich. In **Harry Potter and the Chamber of Secrets** (2002) it is from the front of St Pancras that Harry and his pal Ron take off in their flying blue Ford Anglia.

The hit comedy **Bridget Jones's Diary** (2001) used both King's Cross and St Pancras stations for filming. Early in the film, when Bridget heads off to her parents' home for Christmas, St Pancras is seen covered in (fake) snow. In an early edit of the film, these scenes had much more prominence and can be viewed among the deleted scenes on the DVD version. The deleted scene shows Bridget (Renée Zellweger) walking in front of the snow-covered station. Then, as she boards her train (which was actually shot at King's Cross), she hears voices over the tannoy system and from a nearby vagrant that appear to be commenting on the size of her thighs!

CAMDEN

Camden is one of the most dynamic boroughs of London. Its immensely popular market, which runs from Camden tube station up towards Chalk Farm to the north, is one of the city's most visited tourist attractions. The area is also full of pubs, restaurants and clubs, so it isn't surprising that Camden has proved a popular spot for filming over the years.

The cult favourite **Withnail and I** (1987) was set in Camden Town, but filming actually took place in Notting Hill. The romantic comedy **This Year's Love** (1999), however, directed by David Kane and starring Kathy Burke, Jennifer Ehle and Dougray Scott, was both set and shot in the area, making good use of Camden Lock market, which sits on the Grand Union Canal, and the local pubs and shops. The comedy **The Tall Guy** (1989) was an early screenwriting effort for Richard Curtis, who would go on to script *Four Weddings and a Funeral* (1994) and *Notting Hill* (1999). Starring Jeff Goldblum, Emma Thompson and Rowan Atkinson, the film had the original working title of *Camden Town Boy* and was filmed in and around the area, basing itself at a temporary studio near to Caledonian Road. Also shot at Camden Market and Camden Lock was the engaging romantic comedy **Jack and Sarah** (1995), written and directed by Tim Sullivan, and starring Richard E. Grant and Samantha Mathis.

In Ken Russell's **The Music Lovers** (1970), a surreal biopic of the Russian composer Tchaikovsky (played with verve by Richard Chamberlain), the scene in which the title character attempts suicide was shot at the Grand Union Canal, close to the Gloucester Avenue Bridge near Camden Lock.

The futuristic chiller **Death Machine** (1994), the directorial debut of Stephen Norrington (who would go on to make the Wesley Snipes hit *Blade* (1998)), was shot entirely in the famous London music venue the Roundhouse on Chalk Farm

Road. The old steam repair shed had been a rock venue in the 1960s and 1970s, but in the mid-1990s stood vacant and was the perfect set-cum-location for this horror sci-fi tale of a killer robot. The film starred Brad Dourif and offered an early role for actress Rachel Weisz, who later went on to star in several other London-based films, including *The Mummy Returns* (2001) and *About A Boy* (2002). Writer-director Norrington gave away his cinematic influences when it came to naming characters in the film – they included John Carpenter (played by William Hootkins), Sam Raimi (John Sharian) and (for some reason switched around) one Scott Ridley (Richard Brake).

Camden Lock and the surrounding market make a vibrant location to film in.

TUFNELL PARK

To the south-east of Hampstead and Highgate is the residential area of Tufnell Park, which was used for locations in the drama **Backbeat** (1993), a film that focuses on the tragic story of founder member of The Beatles, Stuart Sutcliffe (Stephen Dorff). The band plays at the Top Ten Club, which is actually The Dome on Dartmouth Park Road. When the band signs a recording deal at the Polydor offices, it is actually a private residential building at nearby High Point, on North Road.

HAMPSTEAD & HIGHGATE

One of the north-west London's most attractive features is Hampstead Heath, a rambling area of woodland and grass that is becoming an increasingly popular spot for film and television companies. Hampstead Heath featured in scenes from the drama **The Boy Who Turned Yellow** (1972), directed by Michael Powell, about a boy on a trip to London. Scenes were shot on the heath itself, as well as at Hampstead tube station and Chalk Farm tube station. The British drama **Wanted for Murder** (1946), starring Eric Portman and Dulcie Gray, also shot on the Hampstead streets.

Kenwood House, a neo-classical mansion that sits among beautifully crafted gardens at the top of the heath, can be spotted in **101 Dalmatians** (1996), and features prominently in one of the crucial scenes in the box-office hit **Notting Hill** (1999). In the scene, William (Hugh Grant) goes to meet Anna (Julia Roberts) on the set of her new period film, which is being shot on location at the stately home. The sequences are all shot on the lawns in front of Kenwood, and make

Elegant Kenwood House on Hampstead Heath can be seen in films such as Notting Hill *(1999), which starred Hugh Grant and Julia Roberts, and* 101 Dalmatians *(1996).*

great use of this attractive and popular spot.

Set in the 1950s, the 1985 drama **Dance with a Stranger** told the story of Ruth Ellis, the last woman to be hanged in Britain. Miranda Richardson gave a searing performance as Ellis, who, in a passionate rage, shot her lover outside the Magdala pub on Hampstead's South Hill. Most of the film was shot in a studio although director Mike Newell did make use of some authentic Hampstead locations, including Well Walk.

William Wyler's thriller **The Collector** (1965), based on the novel by John Fowles, saw Terence Stamp playing a batty butterfly collector who decides to kidnap a student (Samantha Eggar) and add her to his 'collection'. He follows her around Hampstead, and then finally kidnaps her in a scene shot at Mount Vernon Lane off Holly Hill, close to Hampstead tube station. In John Schlesinger's **Darling** (1965) the family home of the television producer (Dirk Bogarde) with whom Diana (Julie Christie) flirts is on South End Road, overlooking Hampstead Heath.

LOCATION LONDON

ACTRESS *Elizabeth Taylor*

DATES *born 1932*

That cinematic great **Elizabeth Taylor** was born at 8 Wildwood Road, Hampstead Heath, on 27 February 1932, to wealthy American parents – her mother was Sara Warmbrodt, a former actress, and her father Francis Taylor a Bond Street art dealer. She lived in the area as a youngster, attending Byron House School in Highgate for two years before she and her family headed off to California just before the outbreak of the Second World War. Her break in the movies came with the 1942 production of *Lassie Come Home*, though stardom came in 1944 when, aged 12, she took the lead role in the equestrian drama *National Velvet*. The rest – the movies, love affairs and multiple marriages – followed swiftly along, though now she has gently settled into the status of movie icon.

Otto Preminger shot his oddball comedy **Bunny Lake is Missing** (1965), starring Laurence Olivier as a copper trying to find the – possibly imaginary – daughter of a woman played by Carol Lynley, around Hampstead. Scripted by John and Penelope Mortimer, the unconventional film also starred Noël Coward as Lynley's landlord. In the film the school that the daughter, Bunny, has vanished from is South Hampstead High School, at 5 Netherhall Gardens, while the climax of the film is staged at Cannon Hall, 14 Cannon Place, off East Heath Road.

In Robert Aldrich's acclaimed and controversial (for its time) drama **The Killing of Sister George** (1968), Beryl Reid played a tough soap star, with Susannah York as her young lover. As the film opens, Reid's character June Buckridge (or Sister George as her soap character is called) drinks at the fictional Marquis of Granby pub – which was in fact the Holly Bush, located at 22 Holly Mount.

The children's film **The Monster of Highgate Ponds** (1961), directed by the great Alberto Cavalcanti and starring Roy Vincente and Ronald Howard, was shot partly in the pretty village of Highgate when there were still ponds at South Green off the High Street. The area is now covered over, but is still called Pond Square.

Highgate Cemetery

Home to the gravestones of many famous – and infamous people – Highgate Cemetery provides a naturally atmospheric and gothic location.

In the stylish – and very amusing – horror film **The Abominable Dr Phibes** (1971), Vincent Price starred as the good doctor who lives in a strange underground world and becomes involved with all sorts of acts of deadly revenge. Though the film was largely shot at Elstree Studios, the scene where Phibes and his wife are laid to rest was shot at Highgate Cemetery in the older section to the west of Swains Lane. Highgate Cemetery also features in a scene from Mike Leigh's **High Hopes** (1988), when Cyril (Philip Davis) and Shirley (Ruth Sheen) go to visit Karl Marx's tomb in the cemetery.

Among the cinematic luminaries buried at the Highgate Eastern Cemetery is much-loved actor **Ralph Richardson** (1902–83). Richardson made more than 60 films during his long career, including *Things To Come* (1936) and *Lady Caroline Lamb* (1972), and is often hailed, along with Laurence Olivier and John Gielgud, as one of the greatest actors of his generation. The film pioneer **William Friese-Greene** (1855–1921) is also buried in Highgate Cemetery, where his gravestone bears the legend 'William Friese-Greene. The inventor of kinematography'. His life story is told in the film *The Magic Box* (1951), which starred Robert Donat as Friese-Greene; though a great pioneer, he died penniless.

Distinguished actress **Gladys Cooper** (1888–1971), who starred in films such as Alfred Hitchcock's *Rebecca* (1940), *Now, Voyager* (1943), *The Bishop's Wife* (1947) and *My Fair Lady* (1964), is buried in another of the areas resting places, Hampstead Cemetery on Fortune Green Road. She was a star on the English stage in the 1930s, but left for Hollywood when offered a small role in Hitchcock's *Rebecca*, and never looked back.

REGENT'S PARK

The refreshing green space of Regent's Park and the famous London Zoo inside it often appear in films. Both can be seen in the delightful comedy **About a Boy** (2002), starring Hugh Grant as Will, a selfish womanizer who preys on single

David Naughton wakes up naked in London Zoo, Regent's Park after a busy night as a werewolf in An American Werewolf in London *(1981).*

mothers. In an early scene he attends a picnic in Regent's Park, and there is a hilarious moment when Will's young companion Marcus (Nicholas Hoult) kills a duck by throwing a loaf of bread at it. In a later scene Will begrudgingly takes Marcus on a trip to London Zoo.

London Zoo was also used as a location in the huge hit **Harry Potter and the Philosopher's Stone** (US title: **Harry Potter and the Sorcerer's Stone** 2001), directed by Chris Columbus. Early in the film, orphan Harry (Daniel Radcliffe), who is unaware of his wizardly powers, is taken to London Zoo by his aunt and uncle, who are his guardians. While in the reptile house he strikes up a conversation with a snake and also unwittingly spirits away the glass keeping the snake in its tank, causing mayhem. London Zoo was also used as a backdrop for a scene in the comedy thriller **Arabesque** (1966), starring Sophia Loren and Gregory Peck, and in a sequence in Carol Reed's drama **The Fallen Idol** (1948), starring Ralph Richardson. In **An American Werewolf in London** (1981), the first time David (David Naughton) metamorphoses into a werewolf, he attacks tramps near to Tower Bridge before moving on to further victims at Aldwych tube station. The next morning sees him waking, naked, in London Zoo.

Regent's Park itself takes an unlikely role in the espionage thriller **Spy Game** (2001), directed by Tony Scott and starring Robert Redford and Brad Pitt. Early in the film Redford's character is summoned from his home in Washington DC to the CIA headquarters in Langley, Virginia. Oddly enough, his route takes him along the Outer Circle road on the outskirts of the park, though obviously driving on the wrong side of the road as he was supposed to be in the US. The attractive white Regency buildings that sit alongside the road can be seen as Redford drives his black Porsche and talks on his mobile phone.

The same Regency buildings were also used as a backdrop for the Hammer chiller **The Nanny** (1965), starring Bette Davis as a psycho-nanny. She is recruited to a smart London house, located on Chester Terrace, which sits adjacent to Regent's Park. The film also stars Wendy Craig, Jill Bennett and James Villiers.

That classic British love story **Brief Encounter** (1954), which was directed by one of the greatest of British directors, David Lean, is rightly most famous for the memorable scenes of the two tentative lovers (beautifully acted by Trevor Howard and Celia Johnson) parting at the railway station. Those scenes were shot at Carnforth Station, Lancashire, but another scene in the film sees the pair in a rowing boat on a boating lake, and this was shot in Regent's Park. In one scene Alec (Howard) is seen stumbling off the end of the boat, clinging onto the Long Bridge at the centre of the Park, before landing knee-deep in the water.

MARYLEBONE

Marylebone Station plays an unusual role in **A Hard Day's Night** (1964). The opening scene, supposedly set in Liverpool, sees the Fab Four heading off to London. This was, in fact, Marylebone Station. Their train ride sees them passing through Paddington and various other stations before arriving – supposedly for the first time – at Marylebone.

In the comedy **Billy Liar** (1963), directed by John Schlesinger, virtually all of the scenes were shot in the north of England, primarily around Bradford where the film is set. The film tells the story of an undertaker's clerk, Billy (Tom Courtenay) who lives in a fantasy world and falls for Liz (Julie Christie). Oddly enough, though, the final scene of Liz leaving for a new life in London from Bradford's Central Station was shot at Marylebone Station. In the chiller **The Day of the Triffids** (1962), in which alien killer plants set about attacking humans, a blinded train driver crashes into Marylebone Station.

Marylebone Station was used for the scene in Lewis Gilbert's charming **Shirley Valentine** (1989) in which Shirley has her passport photograph taken in readiness

Behind the scenes during the filming of Brief Encounter *(1954) on the boating lake in Regent's Park.*

for her holiday escape to Greece. The station can also be seen in a scene from the punk-rock movie starring the Sex Pistols **The Great Rock'n'Roll Swindle** (1980). In the third movie version of John Buchan's adventure novel **The Thirty-Nine Steps** (1978), with Robert Powell as John Hannay, the character of Scudder (John Mills) is killed at Marylebone Station.

KILBURN

In **The Smallest Show on Earth** (1957), Matt and Jean Spenser (Bill Travers and Virginian McKenna) inherit a rundown cinema named the Bijou, and set about trying to transform it from a crumbling fleapit. The cinema itself was built by the film-makers in the space between two railway bridges close to Kilburn tube station. It is a film well worth seeing, both as a delightful comedy and for the wonderfully eccentric performances of Peter Sellers as the projectionist Percy Quill and Margaret Rutherford as pianist Miss Fazackalee.

NORTH-WEST LONDON

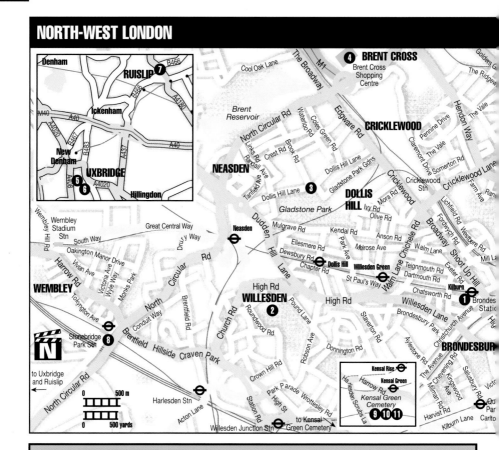

Denham
RUISLIP **7**
B466

Cool Oak Lane
The Broadway
M1
4 BRENT CROSS
Brent Cross
Shopping
Centre
Golders G
The Ridgew

Ickenham
M40
A40

Brent
Reservoir
North Circular Rd
Waterloo Rd
Coles Green Rd
Edgware Rd
CRICKLEWOOD
Pennine Drive
Claremont Drive
The Vale
Somerton Rd
Hendon Way
The Vale

New
Denham
UXBRIDGE
5
6
A4020

Hillingdon

NEASDEN
Links Rd
Crest Rd
Brook Rd
Dollis Hill Lane
Gladstone Park Gdns
Cricklewood
Stn
Cricklewood Lane
Farm Ave
Ran
Tanfield Ave
Randal Ave

Dollis Hill Lane **3**
DOLLIS
HILL
Gladstone Park
Ivy Rd
Mora Rd
Olive Rd
Lichfield Rd
Forwich Rd
Westmere Rd

Wembley
Stadium
Stn
South Way
Great Central Way
Neasden
Dudden Hill Lane
Drury Way
Mulgrave Rd
Kendal Rd
Anson Rd
Chichele Rd
Walm Lane
Shoot Up Hill
Mill La

Oakington Manor Drive
Vivian Ave
Victoria Ave
Wye Way
Monks Park
North Circular Rd
Ellesmere Rd
Dewsbury Rd
Chapter Rd
Park Ave
Melrose Ave
Dollis Hill
Willesden Green
Teignmouth Rd
Dartmouth Rd
Exeter Rd
Broadway

WEMBLEY
Harrow Rd
Tokyngton Ave
Brentfield Rd
St Paul's Way
Walm Lane
Chatsworth Rd
Willesden Lane
Kilburn **1**
Brondes
Static

Stonebridge
Park Stn **8**
Brentfield
Hillside
Craven Park
Conduit Way
High Rd
WILLESDEN **2**
Pound Lane
High Rd
Brondesbury Park
Christchurch Avenue
BRONDESBUR

to Uxbridge
and Ruislip
←
North Circular Rd
0   500 m
0   500 yards
Church Rd
Roundwood Rd
Crown Hill Rd
Park Parade
Wrottesley Rd
Staverton Rd
Robson Ave
Donnington Rd
Aylestone Rd
The Avenue
Clevering Rd
Kingswood Ave
Milman Rd
Salisbury Rd
Victo
Qu
Par

Harlesden Stn
Acton Lane
Station Rd
High St
Willesden Junction Stn
to Kensal
Green Cemetery

Kensal Rise
Kensal Green
Harrow Rd
Hazledon Scrubs La
Kensal Green
Cemetery
9 10 11
Harvist Rd
Kilburn Lane
Carlto

N

LOCATION LONDON

PRODUCER *Lew Grade*

DATES *1906-1998*

Legendary movie impresario **Lew Grade** is buried at the Liberal Jewish Cemetery in Willesden. Born Louis Winogradsky on 25 December 1906 in the Ukrainian town of Tokomak, he emigrated to London aged five with his family. Grade became a professional dancer in his twenties, winning the World Charleston Championships. Later he moved into theatrical management with his brother Bernard Delfont. Through his production company, ITC, Grade produced television programmes such as *The Saint*, *Thunderbirds* and *The Prisoner*. He later started making movies, with a sliding scale of success ranging from the Oscar-winning *On Golden Pond* (1981) to the critically lambasted *Raise the Titanic* (1980).

KEY

1. The Smallest Show on Earth (1957)
2. Babymother (1998)
3. Hellraiser (1987)
4. Tomorrow Never Dies (1997)
5. A Clockwork Orange (1971)
6. Carry On at your Convenience (1971)
7. A Night to Remember (1958)
8. The Man in the White Suit (1951)
9. Theatre of Blood (1973)
10. Morgan, A Suitable Case for Treatment (1966)
11. Look Back in Anger (1959)

The would-be Willesden girl-band led by Anjela Lauren Smith (centre) in Babymother *(1998).*

WILLESDEN

The engaging British musical drama **Babymother** (1998), scripted and directed by Julian Henriques, shot in and around Willesden. It features a great performance by Anjela Lauren Smith as a single mother-of-two struggling to become a singer, and offers a compulsive look at Willesden's young black community.

DOLLIS HILL

Certain exteriors of the gory British horror film **Hellraiser** (1987) were shot in Dollis Hill. Based on Clive Barker's book and directed by the author himself, the film tells of the horrors unleashed when a Chinese puzzle box is opened. The house in which demented Julia Cotton (Clare Higgins) disposes of her victims is actually 187 Dollis Hill Lane (though in the film it is known as 66 Lodovico Street).

BRENT CROSS

The thrilling car-park chase sequence in the James Bond film **Tomorrow Never Dies** (1997), in which Bond (this time played by Pierce Brosnan) manipulates his heavily-armed car by remote control, was shot on the fourth level of the Brent Cross Shopping Centre car-park, close to Golders Green.

UXBRIDGE

When director Stanley Kubrick and his designer John Barry were researching the ideal location to recreate the depressing south-east London suburb of Thamesmead, as presented in Anthony Burgess's 1962 novel *A Clockwork Orange*, they scanned through architectural magazines. They came across the then newly built Brunel University, situated in Uxbridge, which was used for key exteriors in Kubrick's 1971 film adaptation. The university doubled as the fictional Ludovico Medical Facility where Alex (Malcolm McDowell) undergoes gross aversion therapy. Filming also took place on Chelsea Embankment at the now defunct American Drug Store on Chelsea's King's Road and in Thamesmead itself.

On release **A Clockwork Orange** (the film) was deemed controversial for its themes of violence and delinquency and blamed for much copy-cat violence. As a result the film was withdrawn from distribution in Britain for many years under the instructions of Kubrick, but following his death the film was re-released.

Uxbridge can also be seen in the comedy **Carry On at Your Convenience** (1971), which offers up toilet humour in every conceivable way. The film stars the usual crowd, notably Sid James, Kenneth Williams and Joan Sims.

RUISLIP

Of all places, key scenes in **A Night to Remember** (1958), a distinguished account of the Titanic disaster, were shot at Ruislip Lido, Reservoir Road. Superbly directed by Roy Ward Baker, the film starred Kenneth More, Ronald Allen and Honor Blackman, and is a moving and skilful re-telling of the fateful maiden voyage of the *Titanic*. The majority of the scenes were shot at Pinewood Studios, where massive replicas of the Titanic's superstructure were built. However, the studio didn't have a tank large enough for the sequences of the survivors

LOCATION LONDON

PLAYWRIGHT *Terence Rattigan*

DATES *1911-1977*

Screenwriter and playwright **Terence Rattigan** was buried in Kensal Green Cemetery, Harrow Road. Born in Kensington in 1911, he was educated at Oxford. Rattigan famously adapted two of his plays into screenplays – *The Winslow Boy* (1950), which starred Robert Donat, and *The Browning Version* (1951), starring Michael Redgrave. His original screenplays included *The Sound Barrier* (1952), directed by David Lean; *The Prince and the Showgirl* (1957), starring Laurence Oliver and Marilyn Monroe and *Separate Tables* (1958), starring David Niven and Deborah Kerr.

struggling in the sea and on board lifeboats, and so the Ruislip Lido doubled as the freezing North Atlantic.

STONEBRIDGE PARK

The wonderful Ealing comedy **The Man in the White Suit** (1951), which stars Alec Guinness as an inventor who creates a suit made from indestructible material but then finds the textile industry has turned against him, shot largely at the studio, but did do some location filming at Stonebridge Park tube station.

KENSAL GREEN

Kensal Green Cemetery turns up in the witty horror film **Theatre of Blood** (1973), directed by Douglas Hickox. Vincent Price plays actor Edward Lionheart, who, aided by his daughter Edwina (Diana Rigg) vows to kill off the critics who have hammered his performances. Among those killed is Hector Snipe (Dennis Price), whose body is found at Kensal Green Cemetery. The cemetery can also be seen in **Morgan, A Suitable Case for Treatment** (1966), starring David Warner and Vanessa Redgrave, and **Look Back in Anger** (1959) with Richard Burton and Claire Bloom.

NORTH & EAST LONDON

Filming in the north and east of London offers a broad range of urban locations that film-makers are still in the process of discovering. The plots of some films mean that they're obliged to shoot in the area – where else could the film adaptation of Nick Hornby's **Fever Pitch** (1996) be filmed except at Arsenal.

Lurking in the north and east of London are some lovely architectural gems, such as Islington and Muswell Hill, that are ripe for filming. At the other end of the cinematic spectrum, when director Stanley Kubrick saw the disused, ruined Beckton gas works did he see a run-down old factory site? No, he saw war-torn Vietnam!

Arsenal Football Stadium at Highbury is not only revered by Gunners fans, but also by fans of the 1996 film version of Nick Hornby's best-selling novel *Fever Pitch* and the *The Arsenal Stadium Mystery* (1939).

HACKNEY

Richard Attenborough shot his long-planned – and very personal – project **Chaplin** (1992) at a variety of sites around London. In the east end borough of Hackney he recreated scenes of comedian Charlie Chaplin's first comic stage success at the marvellous Hackney Empire on Mare Street.

In the comedy crime thriller **High Heels and Low Lifes** (2001), directed by Mel Smith, Shannon (Minnie Driver) and Frances (Mary McCormack) play best friends who find themselves drawn into the world of bank robberies and gangland villains. They start trying to blackmail a gang of robbers, with an early scene of a disastrous 'cash drop' shot in Hackney's Victoria Park.

STOKE NEWINGTON

A key scene in the erotic-thriller **Killing Me Softly** (2001) was shot at The Castle indoor climbing centre on Green Lanes in Stoke Newington. In one scene, mountaineer Adam (Joseph Fiennes) takes Alice (Heather Graham) to the centre – one of the largest venues for indoor climbing in Europe – to (literally) show her the ropes.

Also shot in Stoke Newington were key sequences from the low-budget BFI production **Young Soul Rebels** (1991), directed by Isaac Julien. Set during the Queen's Silver Jubilee year in 1977, this gay-orientated social drama shot scenes in Stoke Newington's much-loved Clissold Park.

ISLINGTON

On the edge of Islington is the famous Moorfields Eye Hospital on City Road, which was used for key early scenes in the British sci-fi thriller **The Day of the Triffids** (1962), based on John Wyndham's classic novel. After a meteor shower the Earth's inhabitants are left blinded, and therefore rather easy prey to the killer plants, the Triffids. Howard Keel plays Bill Masen, a man recovering from an eye operation at Moorfields who discovers that he is one of the few people left on earth who can see when his bandages are removed.

In **Quadrophenia** (1979), the film based on The Who's album of the same name, the coffee-bar hangout for the Mods (who include Phil Daniels and Sting among their number) was actually the old Art Deco Alfredo's cafe at 4–6 Essex Road,

NORTH-EAST LONDON

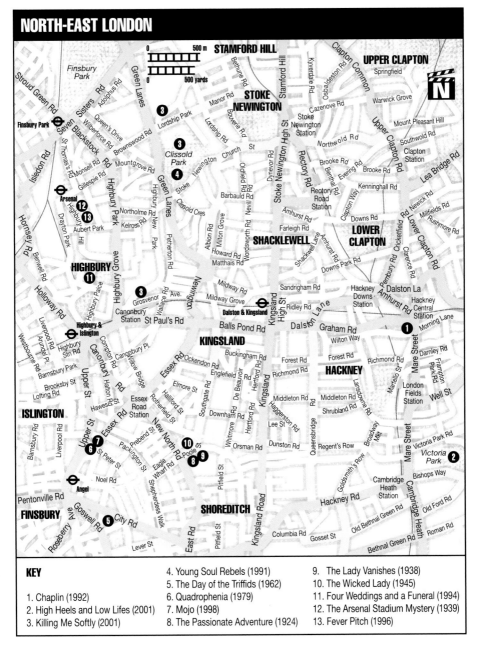

KEY		
	4. Young Soul Rebels (1991)	9. The Lady Vanishes (1938)
	5. The Day of the Triffids (1962)	10. The Wicked Lady (1945)
1. Chaplin (1992)	6. Quadrophenia (1979)	11. Four Weddings and a Funeral (1994)
2. High Heels and Low Lifes (2001)	7. Mojo (1998)	12. The Arsenal Stadium Mystery (1939)
3. Killing Me Softly (2001)	8. The Passionate Adventure (1924)	13. Fever Pitch (1996)

Islington. Closed for many years, but due to be reopened, it can also be seen in Jez Butterworth's **Mojo** (1998), a film starring Ian Hart and Ewan Bremner that looked at the darker side of London in the 1950s.

LOCATION LONDON

DIRECTOR *Sir Alfred Hitchcock*

DATES *1899-1980*

Leytonstone, in east London, was the birthplace of one of cinema's genuine legends. The absolute master of the thriller **Alfred Hitchcock** was born in the living area at the rear of his father's grocery shop at 517 Leytonstone High Road – a site that is now a petrol station. He was schooled at the Jesuit College Saint Ignatius in Stamford Hill, a few miles to the west, and, after initially working as a clerk, became interested in painting.

From here he found his way into the world of cinema as a title-card designer at the Famous Players-Lasky studio in Islington, later to be re-named Gainsborough Studios. He learned about cinema and made his debut as a director with *The Pleasure Garden* (1925). He made the first British talking film *Blackmail* (1929) and went on to establish himself as a master of thrillers in the UK, making *The 39 Steps* (1935) and *The Lady Vanishes* (1938).

After he married his assistant editor Alma Reville he lived at 153 Cromwell Road, west London, until they moved to the USA where Hitchcock achieved even greater fame as a director, making films such as *Rear Window* (1954), *Vertigo* (1958), *North By Northwest* (1959) and *Psycho* (1960).

Gainsborough Studios

By the side of the Grand Union Canal, on the site of a former railway power station in Poole Street, is the site of the famous Gainsborough Film Studios. The power sta-

tion was converted into a film studio in 1891 by the American company Famous Players-Lasky, and many silent films were made there. In 1924 Michael Balcon bought the studios and founded Gainsborough Pictures.

The famous Gainsborough Studios where Alfred Hitchcock made some of his early films.

The first Gainsborough film was *The Passionate Adventure* (1924), scripted by a young Alfred Hitchcock. As a director at the studio, Hitchcock made the comedy-thriller *The Lady Vanishes* (1938), though Gainsborough later became more associated with raunchy – for their time – period melodramas such as *The Wicked Lady* (1945), which starred James Mason and Margaret Lockwood. Rank took over the studio after the Second World War, but it was closed in 1949. In the years that followed it was used for light industrial work, the only hint of its former life being the painted 'Gainsborough Studios' sign on a canal-side wall. Developers have now taken over the site with plans to turn it into residential accommodation, but also with work units and new facilities for film-makers.

HIGHBURY

Scenes from the erotic thriller **Killing Me Softly** (2001) were partially shot in Highbury. In the film Alice (Heather Graham) and her lover Adam (Joseph Fiennes) make passionate love at a London flat that is owned by his sister, Deborah, (Natascha McElhone). The exterior views of the flat were shot at 59 Highbury New Park, a pleasant, tree-shaded residential road that runs from Highbury Grove to Clissold Park, Stoke Newington where the production also shot scenes.

Highbury also appears at the beginning of Mike Newell's **Four Weddings and a Funeral** (1994). Charles (Hugh Grant) and his flatmate, Scarlett (Charlotte Coleman) wake up late and realize that they should be at the first of the four weddings. The flat used was 22 Highbury Terrace, on the edge of Highbury Fields.

Arsenal

One of Highbury's most famous landmarks is Arsenal football ground, home to one of the English football league's most popular, and most successful, football clubs.

No prizes for guessing where the snappily titled **The Arsenal Stadium Mystery** (1939) was set. The film is quite a cult item in certain circles – members of London's National Film Theatre love it. Something of a novelty film, it is about a Scotland Yard Inspector (Leslie Banks) who has to discover who murdered the football team's star player Jack Dyce (Anthony Bushell) during a friendly match. It also provides an opportunity to see members of the 1937–8 championship-winning Arsenal team in a well-directed mystery by Thorald Dickinson – and a chance to view the Arsenal stadium as it once was.

Arsenal was, naturally enough, a vital location for the romantic comedy **Fever Pitch** (1996). Based on Nick Hornby's bestseller about a fanatical Arsenal fan and his struggle to balance romance with his passion for his football team, the film, directed by David Evans, starred Colin Firth as Paul Ashworth, and Ruth Gemmell as Sarah Hughes. Throughout filming, the production found that the local support,

Colin Firth and Ruth Gemmell celebrate Arsenal Football Club's Premiership title with a kiss outside the Arsenal football ground in Fever Pitch *(1996).*

both for Arsenal and for Nick Hornby, proved a huge bonus. Many devout fans of the team provided the authentic football crowd performances, and local residents were extremely accommodating, abiding by full street closures day and night to allow for shooting, and, in particular, for the final street-party scene, which was shot right next to the Arsenal ground.

Fever Pitch was commissioned by David Aukin and Allon Reich of FilmFour, who – in a little test for those working in the film business – can be spotted in crowd scenes shot at the Arsenal ground. The film also used other locations in the north and east, including an Indian restaurant in Brick Lane, Camden Passage in Islington, a pub in Stoke Newington and a school in Muswell Hill.

MUSWELL HILL

Using Fortismere School in Muswell Hill was a particular coup for **Fever Pitch** (1996) as it provided a very convincing location for the school where the characters of Paul (Colin Firth) and Sarah (Ruth Gemmell) teach. Many of the school's pupils appear in the film, both as students in Paul and Sarah's classes, and in the school football team that Paul coaches in a hilarious imitation of his beloved Arsenal's style.

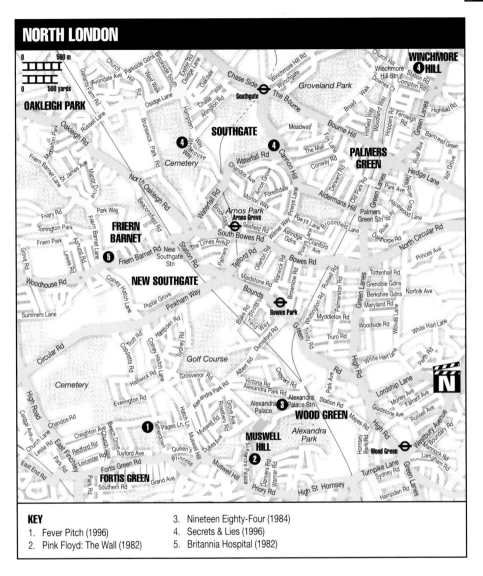

NORTH LONDON

KEY
1. Fever Pitch (1996)
2. Pink Floyd: The Wall (1982)
3. Nineteen Eighty-Four (1984)
4. Secrets & Lies (1996)
5. Britannia Hospital (1982)

Muswell Hill itself was used for a football violence scene in **Pink Floyd: The Wall** (1982), Alan Parker's visualization of prog-rock band Pink Floyd's concept album.

Alexandra Palace

Just east of Muswell Hill, at the top of Alexandra Park, is Alexandra Palace, which has a history that includes it being burnt to cinders twice and also being the home of the BBC's first broadcast. The building became Victory Square in Michael Radford's **Nineteen Eighty-Four** (1984), which starred John Hurt as Winston

LOCATION LONDON

ACTOR *Jack Hawkins*

DATES *1910-1973*

British actor **Jack Hawkins** was born in September 1910 at Lyndhurst Road, Wood Green. He started acting as a youngster, enrolling at the Italia Conti School of Acting in 1922, where his thespian pals included Laurence Olivier and Carol Reed. After the Second World War he signed a contract with producer Alexander Korda, and launched his film career. Fame came after his moving performance in *Mandy* (1953). Later films included the classic wartime drama *The Cruel Sea* (1953), *Ben Hur* (1959) and *Lawrence of Arabia* (1962).

Smith and Richard Burton as O'Brien, Smith's torturer. The film was shot not long after the building had been badly damaged by fire, and it has since been restored.

SOUTHGATE AND WINCHMORE HILL

M ke Leigh shot several prominent scenes from his **Secrets & Lies** (1996) in Southgate. Scenes in the photographic studio run by Maurice (an excellent performance by Timothy Spall) were filmed at a real photographer's studio, The Studio On The Green at 34 The Green, Winchmore Hill. The house Maurice shares with his wife Monica (Phyllis Logan) is nearby at 87 Whitehouse Way in Southgate.

NEW SOUTHGATE

Lindsay Anderson shot **Britannia Hospital** (1982), the final part of his trilogy of films exploring the state of the UK (the other two were **if...** (1968) and **O Lucky Man!** (1973)) at a real – though now closed – hospital. Starring Malcolm McDowell, Leonard Rossiter and Graham Crowden, the film is set in a run-down hospital that

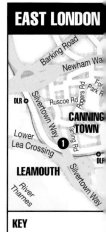

EAST LONDON

Barking Road

Newham Wa

DLR○ Ruscoe Rd

CANNING TOWN

Lower Lea Crossing ❶

LEAMOUTH

River Thames

KEY

is expecting a royal visit, and was filmed at the old Friern Hospital on Friern Barnet Road, in New Southgate.

SILVERTOWN

Mike Hodges set his crime thriller **A Prayer for the Dying** (1987) around the Silvertown area, a part of east London close to the River Thames that is now dominated by City Airport. The film stars Mickey Rourke as Martin Fallon, an IRA killer on the run from his own side who has sworn not to kill again. Also in the cast are Bob Hoskins (as an SAS-man turned priest) and Alan Bates (as an undertaker/Mob boss). Hodges found a disused church in the area for his key showdown scene between Rourke and Bates.

BECKTON

Scenes from Stanley Kubrick's Vietnam War film **Full Metal Jacket** (1987) were famously filmed on land around the derelict Beckton Gas Works on the north side of the Thames in east London, an area that has since been redeveloped. Kubrick refused to fly or leave his home in Britain, so on paper his filming a Vietnam War epic, which included an extensive sequence where US troops battle the Vietnamese during the Tet Offensive in a war-torn town, seemed ludicrous. However, Kubrick

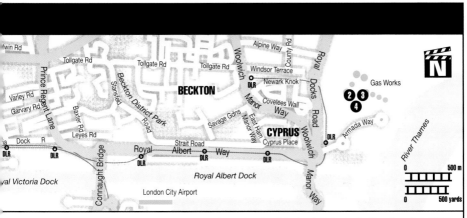

1. A Prayer for the Dying (1987)   2. Full Metal Jacket (1987)   3. Empire of the Sun (1987)   4. For Your Eyes Only (1981)

triumphed. The first section of the film – which stars Matthew Modine, Adam Baldwin and Vincent D'Onofrio – was set in a training camp, with the second part dealing with troops in Vietnam. To recreate the latter scenes, Kubrick and his designer Anton Furst brought in equipment to destroy existing buildings and give them a realistic war-torn look; they imported palm trees from Spain as well as a variety of plastic foliage to give the impression Beckton was the Vietnamese jungle. Kubrick also made do with just two tanks and a couple of helicopters for the action scenes, although one would never guess this when viewing the film.

Following Kubrick's example, Beckton's defunct gas works were used again for another wartime story, this time set in the Second World War – Steven Spielberg's epic drama **Empire of the Sun** (1987). Based on J.G. Ballard's autobiographical novel, it tells the story of a young English boy, Jim (Christian Bale), who is interned by the Japanese in China. Scenes set inside the Japanese detention centre were partly shot at Beckton, though the camp itself – for purposes of the exteriors – was built not in China, but in sunny Spain, near to Jerez.

Beckton also had a role to play in the James Bond film **For Your Eyes Only** (1981), directed by John Glen, with Roger Moore as Bond. The pre-credits sequence sees Bond depositing a wheelchair-bound Blofeld (his nemesis making a brief reappearance) by helicopter into a large industrial chimney on the gas works. The site also crops up in a riot scene in Alan Parker's **Pink Floyd – The Wall** (1982).

Matthew Modine as Private Joker in Stanley Kubrick's Full Metal Jacket *(1987), with the Beckton Gas Works doubling as war-torn Vietnam.*

LOCATION LONDON

ACTRESS *Dame Anna Neagle*

DATES *1904-1986*

ACTRESS *Greer Garson*

DATES *1904-1996*

ACTRESS *Dame Maggie Smith*

DATES *born 1934*

East End Girls

A trio of cinema's finest actresses was born in east London – Dame Anna Neagle, Greer Garson and Dame Maggie Smith.

Dame Anna Neagle

Anna Neagle, one of the UK's best-loved actresses, was born Florence Marjorie Robertson at 3 Park Road, Forest Gate. She began dancing as a child, eventually appearing in various stage productions. Contracted as a film extra at Cricklewood Studios in north London in 1929, she gradually worked her way into higher profile roles, securing a key role alongside Jack Buchanan in *Goodnight Vienna* (1932), and going on to star in a series of major British films including *Nell Gwyn* (1934), *Odette* (1950) and *The Lady with a Lamp* (1951), a biography of Florence Nightingale.

Greer Garson

Hollywood star **Greer Garson** was born at 88 First Avenue, Manor Park in east London, though the Tinseltown publicity machine had her coming from Ireland (she did spend childhood holidays with her grandparents in Co. Down). Her films included *Goodbye Mr Chips* (1939), *Mrs Miniver* (1942), for which she won an Oscar, *Random Harvest* (1942) and *The Forsyte Saga* (1949).

Dame Maggie Smith

The much-loved and highly acclaimed actress **Dame Maggie Smith** was born in the East End at 68 Northwood Gardens, Clayhall, Ilford on December 28, 1934, though at the outbreak of the Second World War the family moved to the outskirts of Oxford. Her distinguished career began when she joined the Oxford Playhouse Company, after which she had success on the West End stage. Her cinema career has been no less notable, with Academy Awards for her performances in *The Prime of Miss Jean Brodie* (1969), a role that she made her own, and *California Suite* (1978). Other films include *A Room With a View* (1985), *The Secret Garden* (1993) and *Gosford Park* (2001).

WEST LONDON

From Notting Hill to Knightsbridge and Paddington to Ealing, the west of London is an area much adored by film-makers, especially in recent years. That being said, the streets of Notting Hill could be seen in many, many movies long before the arrival of Hugh Grant and Julia Roberts in the 1999 romantic comedy that took the area's name. The delightful and somewhat grand buildings around Knightsbridge have also long offered splendid locations, while in Brentford lies Syon House and Park, a stylish stately home popular with film-makers, especially when it comes to the period drama. In days gone by, Ealing was also popular, given its proximity to the legendary studio, which is in the process of being re-launched and could again draw movies into west London.

The busy streets of Notting Hill and Portobello Market are popular location spots with film directors who are aiming to recreate real-life London.

MAIDA VALE

Scenes from the big-screen version of the small-screen sit-com **Man About the House** (1974), which starred Richard O'Sullivan, Paula Wilcox and Sally Thomset, were shot around Maida Vale, with filming also taking place in Shepherd's Bush and St John's Wood. The area also played host to a scene from **Bunny Lake is Missing** (1965) in which a policeman (Laurence Olivier) takes a mother (Carol Lynley) whose daughter is

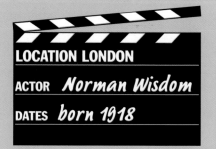

LOCATION LONDON

ACTOR *Norman Wisdom*

DATES *born 1918*

Slapstick comedian **Norman Wisdom** was born in 1918 at 91 Fernhead Road, West Kilburn. After leaving school he worked in a number of jobs, then after the Second World War he decided to try his hand at show business, making his stage debut in Islington in December 1945. He became a star in the West End, and made his movie debut with *Trouble in Store* (1953). He went on to star in a series of comedy vehicles, including *The Square Peg* (1958) and *A Stitch in Time* (1963). Somewhat bizarrely, Wisdom is a huge star in Albania.

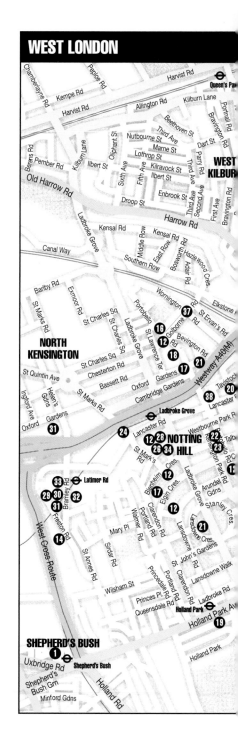

WEST LONDON

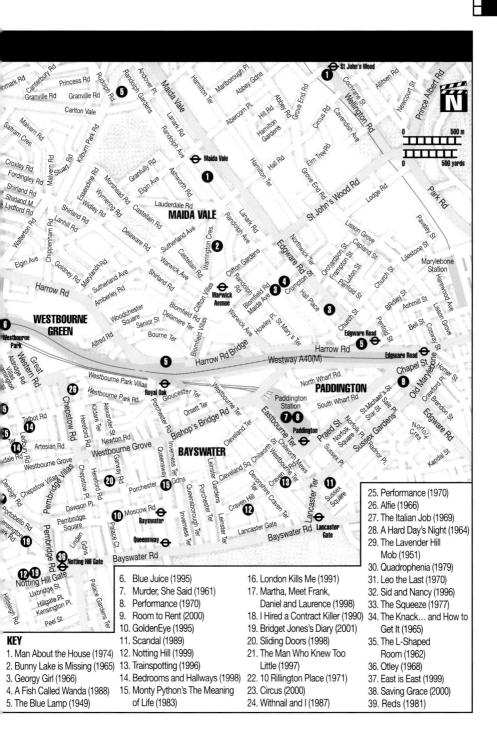

KEY
1. Man About the House (1974)
2. Bunny Lake is Missing (1965)
3. Georgy Girl (1966)
4. A Fish Called Wanda (1988)
5. The Blue Lamp (1949)
6. Blue Juice (1995)
7. Murder, She Said (1961)
8. Performance (1970)
9. Room to Rent (2000)
10. GoldenEye (1995)
11. Scandal (1989)
12. Notting Hill (1999)
13. Trainspotting (1996)
14. Bedrooms and Hallways (1998)
15. Monty Python's The Meaning of Life (1983)
16. London Kills Me (1991)
17. Martha, Meet Frank, Daniel and Laurence (1998)
18. I Hired a Contract Killer (1990)
19. Bridget Jones's Diary (2001)
20. Sliding Doors (1998)
21. The Man Who Knew Too Little (1997)
22. 10 Rillington Place (1971)
23. Circus (2000)
24. Withnail and I (1987)
25. Performance (1970)
26. Alfie (1966)
27. The Italian Job (1969)
28. A Hard Day's Night (1964)
29. The Lavender Hill Mob (1951)
30. Quadrophenia (1979)
31. Leo the Last (1970)
32. Sid and Nancy (1996)
33. The Squeeze (1977)
34. The Knack… and How to Get It (1965)
35. The L-Shaped Room (1962)
36. Otley (1968)
37. East is East (1999)
38. Saving Grace (2000)
39. Reds (1981)

missing for a drink. The pub used was the Warrington Arms, Warrington Crescent.

Just north of the Westway is Maida Avenue, which has featured in several films. In the groovy 1960s comedy-drama **Georgy Girl** (1966), directed by Silvia Narizzamo, the entrance to the pad shared by Charlotte Rampling and Lynn Redgrave was supposed to be Maida Avenue (though actually the flat is at the rear of 449 Edgware Road), while in **A Fish Called Wanda** (1988) it was on Maida Avenue that Michael Palin (and Wanda) lived.

Warren Beatty shot his Oscar-winning drama **Reds** (1981) at a series of locations around the UK – with sections of Liverpool doubling as revolutionary Russia – but he also made use of the Crockers Folly Pub at 24 Aberdeen Place, St John's Wood.

PADDINGTON

The classic British crime film **The Blue Lamp** (1949) – famous for spawning the television series *Dixon of Dock Green* – was the movie that saw the film debut of Dirk Bogarde. It was shot in Paddington Green, though many of the landmarks seen in the film have since vanished. Bogarde played Tom, a masked robber who shoots and kills honest unarmed copper George Dixon (played by Jack Warner, who also played Dixon in the television series). The police station used in the film was the actual Paddington Green Police Station; the blue lamp of the title was retained, and is positioned outside the new station on Harrow Road. The original station was demolished to make way for the Westway flyover, although one site in the film that can be seen still is St Augustine's Church in Kilburn Park Road.

Other nearby locations of *The Blue Lamp* include the Westbourne Terrace Road Bridge over the canal at Little Venice, just north of Paddington – this is where Dixon constructs a poem. Although the site of Bogarde's hideout has since been demolished the area is still recognizable on Lord Hills Road. The Coliseum Cinema where Dixon is shot has since also been destroyed and replaced with council buildings, while the film's tense car chase around west London ends at the old White City dog track off Wood Lane, Shepherd's Bush. This site is now occupied by the BBC's offices.

Westway

The Westway flyover – the main road through west London – can be glimpsed in the comedy drama **Blue Juice** (1995), that rarest of films, a British surf movie! Though the majority of the film, which stars Sean Pertwee and Catherine Zeta Jones, was shot in Cornwall, early scenes see characters played by Ewan McGregor and Stephen Mackintosh 'kidnap' their buddy (Peter Gunn) and drag him down to the coast for a little fun in the surf. An overhead shot pans over the Westway and down to a pub outside which the pair lurk before making off with their pal.

Paddington Station

Paddington railway station provided a backdrop in **Murder, She Said** (1961), an adaptation of one of Agatha Christie's Miss Marple mysteries which starred Margaret Rutherford as the prim detective. Given that the original title of the book was *4.50 From Paddington* it is none too surprising that director George Pollock used the station. The station can also be seen in **Performance** (1970), with James Fox grabbing a waiting cab under the station arches.

Edgware Road

The comedy **Room to Rent** (2000) was shot at a variety of London locations, including Soho and the Arab-influenced district of Edgware Road. Directed by Khaled El Hagar, the film stars Said Taghmaoui as a young Egyptian living in London and American actress Juliette Lewis as the Marilyn Monroe impersonator with whom he gets involved. Producer Ildiko Kemeny said: 'Whilst it was a challenge to shoot on location, especially in Soho and the Edgware Road, it was definitely worth it. I love our title sequence. It's a wonderful display of exotic colours, people and Arabic signs which make you feel that you must be in an Arabic city. Suddenly a red double-decker bus cuts through the action and you realize that you must be in London. It's fantastic for Londoners to have access to all these different cultures.'

> '**I**t's a wonderful display of exotic colours, people and Arabic signs which make you feel that you must be in an Arabic city … It's fantastic for Londoners to have access to all these different cultures.'
>
> ILDIKO KEMENY, PRODUCER, *ROOM TO RENT*

BAYSWATER

In the James Bond film **GoldenEye** (1995), directed by Martin Campbell and starring Pierce Brosnan as 007, much of the film was set in Russia. Although some filming took place in Russia, many locations in the UK substituted. During the course of the film, Bond meets up with Natalya (Izabella Scorupco) in a St Petersburg church, though this was actually St Sofia's Greek Cathedral on Moscow Road, Bayswater.

Scandal (1989), directed by Michael Caton-Jones, told the story of the Profumo Affair, which had a massive impact on British politics in the 1960s. Joanne Whalley played Christine Keeler, whose relationship both with cabinet minister John Profumo (Ian McKellen) and a Russian attaché influenced the collapse of the Tory government in 1963. John Hurt played Stephen Ward, the shallow middleman who 'introduced'

Keeler to men. Ward eventually committed suicide, having been charged with living off immoral earnings. In reality Ward lived at 17 Wimpole Mews, Marylebone, though the film shot the scenes of his flat at 42 Bathurst Mews, Bayswater.

Naturally enough, **Notting Hill** (1999) shot many of its scenes in the west London area, the wedding reception at the close of the film being set in the lovely garden of designer Anouska Hempel's Hempel Hotel, on Craven Hill. Another hugely successful, but vastly different, British film was the cult classic **Trainspotting** (1996), most of which was shot in Scotland, where it was set. However, the film's final scenes deal with some of the characters on a trip to London. The exterior of the hotel in which a drug deal is planned is the Royal Eagle Hotel, Craven Road.

Many key scenes from Rose Troche's romantic comedy **Bedrooms and Hallways** (1998) were shot in Bayswater. The film, which stars Kevin McKidd, Jennifer Ehle and Simon Callow, shot at Coins Coffeé House on Talbot Road, at the Leslie Marsh Estate Agents on Ledbury Road and at nearby Ladbroke Square Gardens and Freston Road in Notting Hill.

Queensway

A memorable scene from **Monty Python's The Meaning of Life** (1983) was shot at the Porchester Halls, Queensway. In the scene, the disgustingly obese Mr Creosote, lustily played by Terry Jones in an extremely large fat suit, explodes after having one mouthful of food too many – it is a tiny wafer-thin mint that proves crucial.

NOTTING HILL

Notting Hill – The Movie

Notting Hill is a culturally diverse, hip and highly desirable area, famous for its annual carnival. The film that is most associated with Notting Hill is, of course, the 1999 romantic comedy that takes its name. Fans of the movie from around the world can take part in *Notting Hill* walks around Portobello Road and the surrounding streets, with guides pointing out locations from the film. Directed by Roger Michell, **Notting Hill** (1999) is a witty piece of romantic fluff in which Hollywood movie star Anna Scott (charmingly played by Julia Roberts) walks into the travel bookshop owned by William Thacker (Hugh Grant). They gradually fall in love, and the film charts the ups and downs of their relationship. The film also featured a striking and utterly hilarious performance by Rhys Ifans as Thacker's grungy flatmate Spike.

William (Hugh Grant), Anna (Julia Roberts) and Spike (Rhys Ifans) discuss love and life round William's kitchen table in Notting Hill *(1999)*

'Notting Hill is a melting pot and the perfect place to set a film.'

RICHARD CURTIS,
SCREENWRITER,
NOTTING HILL

Notting Hill's screenwriter Richard Curtis (who had previously scripted *Four Weddings and a Funeral* (1994)), once lived in Notting Hill. He said: 'Notting Hill is an extraordinary mixture of cultures. It seemed a proper and realistic place where people from different worlds could actually meet and co-exist – that Anna would be shopping there, that William would live and work there and that Spike might think it was a groovy place to hang out and dwell in.'

The film-makers wanted to make good use of the Portobello Road, where the fictional bookshop is located, and therefore had to juggle the practical realities of filming in a busy urban area. The house with the blue door where William Thacker lives in the film is actually 280 Westbourne Park Road, and was once owned by Richard Curtis. The blue door itself is no longer there as it was auctioned off for the princely sum of £9,300 in 2000. William's bookshop is actually Nicholls Antique Arcade at 142 Portobello Road, which had to be dressed to look like a bookshop. However, at nearby 13 Blenheim Crescent, the actual travel bookshop on which it was based can be seen.

Anna and William can be seen watching a film at Notting Hill's Coronet Cinema, with William, for complicated reasons, wearing a scuba-diving mask. The restaurant that is William's friend's failed business is actually Portfolio, an art store at the junction of Bevington Road and Golborne Road. It was also used as a diner in Hanif Kureishi's film **London Kills Me** (1991), another film that used the Notting Hill streets.

The lovely private gardens that William and Anna climb into after dinner at friends, and that we see in the last frame of the film, are actually Rosmead Gardens in Rosmead Road.

Notting Hill – The Place

Beyond its eponymous film, many other movies, both British- and US-made, have made use of the Notting Hill environs. The romantic comedy, **Martha, Meet Frank, Daniel and Laurence** (1998), shot at Mike's Cafe on Blenheim Crescent in Notting Hill for early scenes in which Frank (Rufus Sewell) and Laurence (Joseph Fiennes) get together, and on the Portobello road. The Warwick Castle pub in Portobello Road was used as a location in the comedy thriller **I Hired a Contract Killer** (1990), directed by Aki Kaurismaki, and starring Margi Clarke and Jean-Pierre Leaud.

To prepare for her role in **Bridget Jones's Diary** (2001), American star Renée Zellweger went 'undercover' for two and a half weeks as a dogsbody at London publishers Picador under the alias of 'Bridget Cavendish' to help master her British accent and get used to the working environment. Over the period she answered phones and made photocopies and cups of coffee. Zellweger also had to transform herself physically and gained a substantial amount of weight to play the calorie-counting obsessive Bridget. Hugh Grant appeared as her caddish boss Daniel Cleaver, with Colin Firth as his romantic rival Mark Darcy.

Much of the filming took place around Notting Hill, as well as in Holland Park and St James's Square. Notting Hill restaurants featured in the film include trendy spots such as Pharmacy and 192, as well as a local branch of Coffee Republic.

Sliding Doors (1998) also shot in the area. In the film Helen (Gwyneth Paltrow) shares a house with Gerry (Jon Lynch) – this is at 62 Princes Square – while filming also took place at Mas Cafe, All Saints Road in Notting Hill.

The Hitchcock spoof **The Man Who Knew Too Little** (1997) shot at various places in Notting Hill. Directed by Jon Amiel, the film has funnyman Bill Murray as a naïve American who becomes entangled in an assassination plot while under the mistaken impression that he is taking part in a participatory group drama. The film – which also stars Joanne Whalley – shot in Lansdowne Crescent, St Luke's Road, the corner of Portobello Road and Raddington Road and at the Acklam Road railway footbridge close to the Westway.

The Electric Cinema in Notting Hill featured in 10 Rillington Place (1971) and Circus (2000).

The Electric Cinema on Portobello Road was a prominent location in the crime drama **10 Rillington Place** (1971) with Richard Attenborough as the real-life mass-murderer John Christie. The film shot in Rillington Place itself, before the notorious street was demolished and renamed, becoming Rushton Mews. The Electric Cinema was also used as a location for the crime drama **Circus** (2000), starring Eddie Izzard and John Hannah, although most of the film was shot in Brighton.

The cult 1960s-set comedy **Withnail and I** (1987), which starred Richard E. Grant and Paul McGann filmed most of its early scenes in Notting Hill, which stood in for Camden Town where the film was actually set. The film's fictional Mother Black Cap pub is actually Fudrucker's on Lancaster Road at St Mark's Grove, while filming also took place at the old wolf enclosure in London Zoo.

Performance (1970), which cast Mick Jagger as a has-been rock star and James Fox as a small-time hood, was thought to be a failure initially, but has since gone on to achieve cult status and is certainly a stunning film to watch. Directed by Nicolas Roeg and Donald Camell, the film was shot at the close of the Swinging

Leslie Caron outside her dowdy west London boarding house in The L-Shaped Room *(1962).*

Sixties. Fox plays a mobster on the run who hides in the home of Jagger's fallen rocker and is drawn into a seedy world of sex, drugs and mysticism. The address of the house given in the film is 81 Powis Square, but the actual exterior is 25 Powis Square, just off Ledbury Road.

In **Alfie** (1966), the seedy bedsit where Michael Caine's Alfie lives is 22 St Stephen's Gardens, off the Chepstow Road. In the film both Caine and Jane Asher, who plays one of Alfie's many paramours, can be seen in Notting Hill, while the film also shot at a variety of locations around London. Michael Caine made a return visit to the area a few years later when filming the comedy caper **The Italian Job** (1969), in which, as Charlie Croker, he took a team off to Turin in Italy to stage a daring robbery using three Minis and a bus. At the beginning of the film, when Croker has just been released from prison, he returns to his trendy flat, which is located at 18 Denbigh Close.

One of the most memorable cinematic images of the 1960s – The Beatles are chased through the streets by hordes of fans – came from **A Hard Day's Night** (1964) and was shot in Notting Hill. The film's director Richard Lester said that shooting street exteriors when the group was so popular was extremely difficult. He recalled: 'Basic logistics were impossible. As soon as I had them run to their marks and do a scene, 2,000 crazed fans would appear, popping up out of manhole covers. Then the police would crash down and say "Piss off!", and we'd have to find another location and do take two.'

The climax of the London chase sequence in the classic Ealing comedy **The Lavender Hill Mob** (1951), which starred Alec Guinness and Stanley Holloway, took place at the Bramley Arms pub in Notting Hill. The pub was also used in **Quadrophenia** (1979), directed by Franc Roddam, and John Boorman's drama **Leo the Last** (1970), which starred Marcello Mastroianni as Leo, a convalescent aristocrat who sets up home in Notting Hill and becomes acquainted with the locals who rent his properties; the film also shot at the

Westway Sports Centre on Bramley Road. Bramley Road can also be seen in the punk-rock biopic **Sid and Nancy** (1996), which starred Gary Oldman and Chloe Webb in the title roles, and in the crime film **The Squeeze** (1977), starring Stacey Keach and James Fox.

Street scenes for the comedy **The Knack... and How to Get It** (1965) also used Notting Hill as a location, as did another 1960s movie, **The L-Shaped Room** (1962). Starring Leslie Caron as Jane, an unmarried mother, and based on the novel by Lynne Reid Banks, *The L-Shaped Room* shot in several places around the area, using 4 St Luke's Road as the unpleasant boarding house Jane lodges in. Meanwhile, Notting Hill Gate tube station crops up in the spy spoof **Otley** (1968), directed by Dick Clement, which features Tom Courtenay as a hapless petty criminal caught up in the world of espionage.

The Earl of Warwick pub at Golborne Road was used for scenes in the hit British comedy **East is East** (1999), directed by Damien O'Donnell, and starring Im Puri and Linda Bassett. Portobello Road can also be seen in the comedy **Saving Grace** (2000), which featured Brenda Blethyn as a middle-class marijuana producer who travels from her West Country home to try and sell drugs in the Notting Hill streets.

EARLS COURT

The cult horror film **An American Werewolf in London** (1981) made great use of locations in central London, but Earls Court also had a part to play. In the film, David (David Naughton) is attacked by a werewolf while visiting the Yorkshire Moors. He recovers in the Princess Beatrice Maternity Hospital on Finborough Road, tended by a friendly nurse Alex Price (Jenny Agutter), which was the Princess Beatrice Maternity Hospital on Finborough Road. Price's flat (where David transforms into a werewolf in one scene) is at nearby 64 Coleherne Road.

The interiors of the royal palace in Richard Loncraine's **Richard III** (1995), were actually a subtle blending of St Cuthbert's Church in Philbeach Gardens, Earls Court – seen mainly in the musical sequence – and the Holbein Room of Strawberry Hill House, Twickenham.

In Iain Softley's 1997 adaptation of *The Wings of the Dove*, Kate Croy (Helena Bonham Carter) goes to look after her mother's grave at Brompton Cemetery, located at Old Brompton Road, Earls Court. The cemetery can also be seen in Mark Peploe's psychological thriller **Afraid of the Dark** (1991), which starred James Fox, Fanny Ardant and Paul McGann.

The apartment block where Belgian manicurist Carol Ledoux (Catherine Deneuve) lives in Roman Polanski's impressive and macabre psychological thriller **Repulsion** (1965) is actually Kensington Mansions on Trebovir Road, located behind Earls Court tube station.

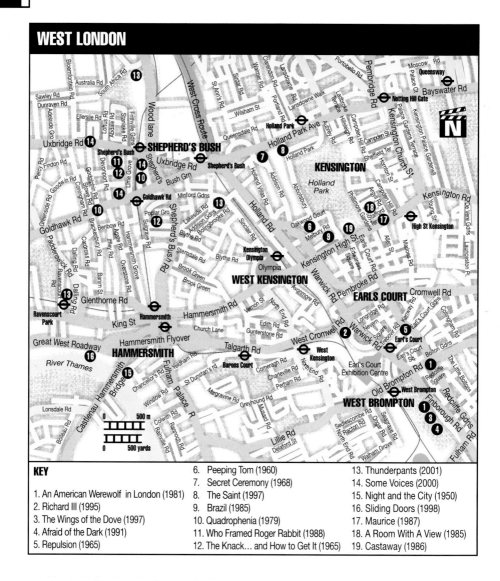

WEST LONDON

KEY

1. An American Werewolf in London (1981)
2. Richard III (1995)
3. The Wings of the Dove (1997)
4. Afraid of the Dark (1991)
5. Repulsion (1965)

6. Peeping Tom (1960)
7. Secret Ceremony (1968)
8. The Saint (1997)
9. Brazil (1985)
10. Quadrophenia (1979)
11. Who Framed Roger Rabbit (1988)
12. The Knack… and How to Get It (1965)

13. Thunderpants (2001)
14. Some Voices (2000)
15. Night and the City (1950)
16. Sliding Doors (1998)
17. Maurice (1987)
18. A Room With A View (1985)
19. Castaway (1986)

KENSINGTON

Scenes from Michael Powell's disturbing chiller **Peeping Tom** (1960) were shot in Holland Park. The film stars Carl Boehm as Mark Lewis, the deeply disturbed son of a vicious filmmaker, who gets his kicks by filming the terror in women's faces as he murders them. The opening scenes take place in Fitzrovia, though Lewis's home is actually 5 Melbury Road, off High Street Kensington. Ironically, director Michael Powell – who also plays Boehm's sadistic father – lived just across the road at 8 Melbury Road, and used his own garden to shoot the film's home movie footage of Mark as a young boy (actually the footage showed Powell and his son). The film was much criticized on its initial release and for a long time ruined Powell's reputation, though it has since been re-evaluated and is now regarded as something of a masterpiece.

Nearby is the house where Joseph Losey filmed the drama **Secret Ceremony** (1968), starring Elizabeth Taylor, Robert Mitchum and Mia Farrow. The house itself is very much a character in this twisted morality tale. Allegedly, Losey was fascinated with this Gothic house and saw it as the perfect location for his strange psycho-drama. The look of the house, with its odd tall chimneys and distinct turquoise tiles, added much to the film's drama. The majority of the film was shot at the house on 8 Addison Road, apart from a few interiors shot at a studio and a brief location trip to Noordmeyer on the Dutch coast.

In Philip Noyce's **The Saint** (1997), with Val Kilmer as a 1990s version of Simon Templar, the London hotel in which Templar stays (before his room in invaded by gun-wielding thugs) is actually the Halcyon Hotel at 81 Holland Park, a hotel actually much frequented by those in the film industry.

Terry Gilliam's cult fantasy thriller **Brazil** (1985), a complex tale about a futuristic bureaucratic world with Jonathan Pryce as Sam, a harassed clerk who becomes a reluctant hero, was shot at a variety of locations around London. Sam's mother (Katharine Helmond) has regular facial alterations, and the location used for her surgery is in fact the Arab Hall of Leighton House, 12 Holland Park Road.

The Merchant Ivory team has made excellent use of the Linley-Sambourne house at 18 Stafford Terrace: the building featured in both **A Room With a View** (1985) and **Maurice** (1987). In *A Room With a View* it is the home of Cecil Vyse (Daniel Day Lewis), while in *Maurice* it acts as the London home of Clive Durham (Hugh Grant). A beautiful Victorian house, it is open to the public on certain days of the week.

Though the majority of Nic Roeg's **Castaway** (1986), which starred Oliver Reed and Amanda Donohoe as a strange pairing who go and live on a South Seas island, was clearly not shot in the UK, some early scenes were based in London. In the film, Gerald (Reed) advertises for a woman to come and live on the island with him and Lucy (Donohoe) replies. She is working in a tax office – shot at Charles House, High Street Kensington – so it is easy to see why the South Seas sounded more appealing.

SHEPHERD'S BUSH

Rock band The Who came from the Shepherd's Bush area, so it seemed natural that when it came to recreating the band's album **Quadrophenia** (1979) for the big

> '**S**hepherd's Bush is one of those chunks of London that everyone knows. It has many guises: it can be quite bright and glamorous, or quite rough and hard or even very mundane and quiet.'
>
> SIMON CELLAN JONES,
> DIRECTOR *SOME VOICES*

screen that filming should take place around the same west London streets. Set in the 1960s, the film dealt with the tussles between the scooter-riding Mods and motorbike-riding Rockers, and starred Phil Daniels as the parka-clad Mod Jimmy Michael Cooper. The film, directed by Franc Roddam, has scenes of Jimmy riding his multi-mirrored scooter along the Goldhawk Road and being attacked in Shepherd's Bush Market. The film also starred Ray Winstone, Sting, Toyah Wilcox and Leslie Ash.

The ingenious comedy **Who Framed Roger Rabbit?** (1988), which managed to blend live action with animation, was shot largely north of London at Elstree Studios in Hertfordshire. Set in Los Angeles, it is the story of 1930s private eye Eddie Valiant (Bob Hoskins) who ends up trying to prove the innocence of Roger, a cartoon rabbit accused of murder. Most exterior locations were shot in Los Angeles, but the Acme factory that can be seen in some of the key final scenes is actually an empty electrical testing station in Shepherd's Bush.

The Knack… and How to Get It (1965), directed by Richard Lester and starring Rita Tushingham and a young Michael Crawford, shot street scenes around Shepherd's Bush, while scenes in the film's 'white pad' were shot at nearby 1 Melrose Terrace.

The British children's comedy **Thunderpants** (2001) – so named due to the ability of its lead character, youngster Patrick Smash (Bruce Cook), to break wind with enormous power – was partly shot around Shepherd's Bush. The exterior of Smash's school was actually Addison Gardens in Shepherd's Bush, while the interior was in reality Burlington Danes School in White City. The nursery used was in nearby Ravenscourt Park.

In **Some Voices** (2000), Daniel Craig plays a man released from a psychiatric hospital who returns to London in order to rehabilitate from his illness. He is helped by his restaurateur brother (David Morrissey) and supported by prescription drugs. He meets and falls for Laura (a fine performance by Kelly MacDonald, whose first film was *Trainspotting*), but his condition gradually slips as, denying himself his medication, he tries to embrace life.

The director of *Some Voices*, Simon Cellan Jones, was able to have a two-week rehearsal period with the actors in the Shepherd's Bush, where the film is largely located. As part of his preparation for his role as a hard-working restaurateur, actor David Morrissey actually worked in the café where the film was shot. Both Cellan Jones and actor Daniel Craig also live in the area. Cellan Jones commented: 'Shepherd's Bush is one of those chunks of London that everyone knows. It has

Gwyneth Paltrow and John Hannah patronized Hammersmith's Blue Anchor for a scene in the 1998 romantic comedy Sliding Doors.

many guises: it can be quite bright and glamorous, or quite rough and hard or even very mundane and quiet.'

The production shot on both the Goldhawk Road and Uxbridge Road, and also, to the amusement of passers by, in Shepherd's Bush Market. 'Shooting on a busy road, people noticed us and every now and again you would get people looking into the camera and yelling, but we would just have to let it go. Sometimes we got wonderful stuff and other times we would have to re-shoot as someone would come out of a pub and start yelling at us.'

HAMMERSMITH

In a sinister scene from Jules Dassin's **Night and the City** (1950), Richard Widmark's Harry comes to a sticky end and is dumped into the Thames at Hammersmith under the watchful eye of Kristo, a role played with suitable menace by Herbert Lom.

In a lighter vein, the romantic comedy **Sliding Doors** (1998) traces the two possible lives for a woman (Gwyneth Paltrow) after she loses her job. In one scene Paltrow and her prospective lover, James (John Hannah), engage in a little relaxing rowing along the Thames near to Lower Mall, Hammersmith, and the pair also take a drink at The Blue Anchor, 13 Lower Mall, Hammersmith.

WEST LONDON

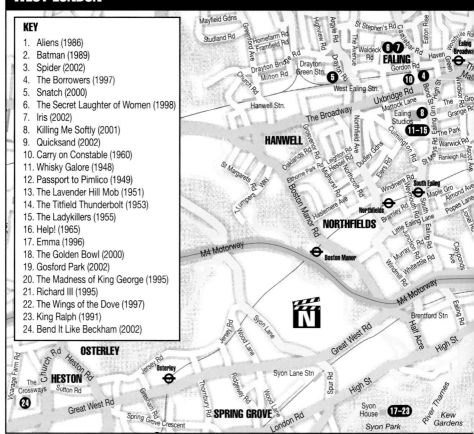

KEY

1. Aliens (1986)
2. Batman (1989)
3. Spider (2002)
4. The Borrowers (1997)
5. Snatch (2000)
6. The Secret Laughter of Women (1998)
7. Iris (2002)
8. Killing Me Softly (2001)
9. Quicksand (2002)
10. Carry on Constable (1960)
11. Whisky Galore (1948)
12. Passport to Pimlico (1949)
13. The Lavender Hill Mob (1951)
14. The Titfield Thunderbolt (1953)
15. The Ladykillers (1955)
16. Help! (1965)
17. Emma (1996)
18. The Golden Bowl (2000)
19. Gosford Park (2002)
20. The Madness of King George (1995)
21. Richard III (1995)
22. The Wings of the Dove (1997)
23. King Ralph (1991)
24. Bend It Like Beckham (2002)

LOCATION LONDON

DIRECTOR *Carol Reed*

DATES *1906-1976*

The acclaimed British director **Carol Reed** is buried at Kensington Cemetery, Gunnersbury Avenue, just north of the river. Born in Putney, he started as a young actor but later realized his skills lay behind the camera rather than in front of it. His first film as a director was *Midshipman Easy* (1934), and he went on to direct such classics as *Odd Man Out* (1946), *The Third Man* (1949) and *Oliver!* (1968).

ACTON

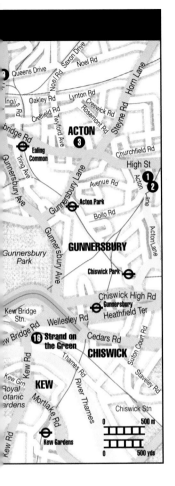

Though you would never really know it to watch the film, scenes from the science-fiction chiller **Aliens** (1986), directed by James Cameron, were filmed in Acton. Set way in the future, Cameron's follow-up to the original *Alien* (1979) saw Ripley (Sigourney Weaver) team up with a band of gung-ho space marines and head off to a factory complex on a distant planet to slug it out with a horde of nasty aliens. Cameron shot the film primarily at Pinewood Studios, but for certain factory scenes the film also shot at the vast disused Acton Lane Power Station. The same power station was used in **Batman** (1989), directed by Tim Burton, for the scenes in which Jack Nicholson falls into a vat of chemicals after being shot by the police. Nicholson emerges transformed into the white-faced villain, the Joker.

In **Spider** (2002) the working-class house of the title character's parents is located at a row of nineteenth-century railway cottages alongside disused railway yards in Acton.

EALING

Ealing Town Hall was used in the fantasy adventure **The Borrowers** (1997), which starred John Goodman and Jim Broadbent, with the building doubling – appropriately enough – as a town hall. Guy Ritchie's crime film **Snatch** (2000), which featured Brad Pitt and Vinnie Jones, also shot in the area, with scenes filmed at Jester's Amusement Arcade in West Ealing. Ealing was also used as a backdrop in the drama **The Secret Laughter of Women** (1998), which starred Colin Firth and Nimi Da Silva.

Scenes from the moving drama **Iris** (2002), which reflected upon the life of the novelist Iris Murdoch and starred Judi Dench and Jim Broadbent, were filmed in Ealing, while Ealing Green also featured in the thriller **Killing Me Softly** (2001). Another film from the same genre, **Quicksand** (2002), starring Michael Keaton and Michael Caine, was filmed around Hanger Lane, Ealing. On a lighter note, Ealing town centre can also be seen in the classic British comedy **Carry on Constable**

(1960), the fourth in the Carry On series, and – as usual – starring Sid James and Kenneth Williams.

Ealing Studios

The famous Ealing Studios were established at Ealing Green by Will Barber in 1902, and provided a production base for many films in the 1930s. When Michael Balcon took over the studio in 1938 it became really successful, attracting talents such as directors Charles Crichton, Sandy Mackendrick and Alberto Cavalcanti. Ealing developed a sterling reputation for comedies during the 1940s and 1950s, making films such as *Whisky Galore* (1948), *Passport to Pimlico* (1949), *The Lavender Hill Mob* (1951), *The Titfield Thunderbolt* (1953) and *The Ladykillers* (1955).

Ealing Studios was the power-house of British comedy in the 1950s; the site is now being regenerated.

The Studios were sold to the BBC in 1955 when the production company switched its base to Pinewood Studios. The BBC made active use of the studio for almost 40 years, but it was then passed on to the National Film and Television School. In mid-2000, Ealing Studios was acquired by a company with a background in film, technology and estate development, which has plans to develop the site into a film and new technology studio for the 21st century.

BRENTFORD

Strand-on-the Green

The Beatles were in the Brentford area for their second film **Help!** (1965). As with *A Hard Day's Night*, *Help!* was directed by Richard Lester, and a memorable scene was shot at the City Barge riverside pub at 27 Strand-on-the-Green, just east of Kew Bridge. The pub in the film features a stuffed tiger in the basement, which sadly is no longer there.

Syon House

With 200 landscaped acres of parkland edging onto the River Thames, Syon House is the London home of the Duke of Northumberland. This exquisite mansion has regularly featured as a period location, playing host to a series of highly acclaimed costume dramas. These include John McGrath's **Emma** (1996), starring Gwyneth Paltrow as the eponymous heroine; **The Golden Bowl** (2000), directed by James Ivory and starring Uma Thurman and Kate Beckinsale; **Gosford Park** (2002), directed by Robert Altman and featuring a stellar British cast, including Maggie Smith, Michael Gambon and Helen Mirren; **The Madness of King George** (1995), starring Nigel Hawthorne and Helen Mirren, again; **Richard III** (1995), with Ian McKellen; **The Wings of the Dove** (1997), starring Helena Bonham Carter. Another totally different sort of film that was shot there was the comedy **King Ralph** (1991), starring John Goodman as a Yank who becomes the King of England.

The romantic Syon House has made a perfect backdrop for many period movies.

HESTON

The premise of the charming film **Bend It Like Beckham** (2002) sees 18-year-old Jess (Parminder Nagra) desperate to play football like her hero, Manchester United star David Beckham. However, her parents just want her to be a nice conventional Indian girl. Jess meets Jules (Keira Knightley) who invites her to join the local women's football team, leading to a comedy about the dreams and aspirations of the two girls, both of whom want far more than the dictates of their upbringings. Scenes of the house where Jess and her family live were shot at Sutton Square in Heston, while the film also shot at Southall and Piccadilly Circus.

Directed by Gurinder Chadha – who also made the comedy *Bhaji on the Beach* (1993) – the film features the acting debut of singer Shaznay Lewis who once fronted girl group All Saints; Lewis appears as the team captain.

SOUTH-WEST LONDON

The south-west of London offers a broad range of options for film-makers – within a few miles they can shoot the plush opulence of Belgravia and Chelsea and still make an easy leap to the grittier streets of Brixton and Wandsworth. The proximity to studios in Twickenham also makes the outer edges of the south-west a popular shooting location, though the Heathrow flight path has been known to cause problems over the years for various productions. Barnes offers wonderful access to the River Thames, while Richmond has stunning parkland. The area also includes a fine selection of museums and impressive architecture, such as the Royal Albert Hall and the Natural History Museum in Kensington. In fact, south-west London is a film-maker's dream.

The Thames at Richmond and Barnes (Richmond Bridge shown here) has featured in many films, including *Shakespeare in Love* (1998), starring Joseph Fiennes and Gwyneth Paltrow.

WESTMINSTER

With landmarks that include the Houses of Parliament and Westminster Abbey, this is an area that often appears in films, though it usually tends to feature more as a cursory backdrop than as a fleshed-out scene. This is possibly due to the hassle, confusion and security nightmare that would involve a film crew taking over the roads around Britain's seat of government.

In **102 Dalmatians** (2000), a follow-up to the successful UK-shot live-action version of *101 Dalmatians*, Glenn Close again plays Cruella de Vil. The evil puppy torturer has recently been released from prison and is declared cured following pioneering behaviour-control therapy. Now a changed woman, she decides to spend her time investing in – and helping at – the flailing Second Chance Dogs Home, much to the amazement of her parole officer. However, Cruella's therapy misfires, and she is restored to her evil self. Suddenly, cute little Dalmatian puppies start vanishing from London homes. As in the previous film, Dalmatian owners (this time played by Ioan Gruffudd and Alice Evans) rush to the rescue aided by a few animal friends.

Though the climax to the film is set in Paris, Westminster's Big Ben plays a vital role in the film. The office of Cruella's parole officer is situated directly opposite the Houses of Parliament, and it is the noise of Big Ben striking that causes Cruella's therapy to fail. In one stunning sequence – achieved largely thanks to computer special effects – Cruella thinks she sees the Houses of Parliament, buses, cars, people and even Westminster Bridge bearing the distinctive black-and-white Dalmatian markings. In a similar special-effects technique, the Houses of Parliament appear to be covered with blankets of snow in a scene from **The Avengers** (1998).

The comedy **Ali G Indahouse** (2002) also used the Houses of Parliament in several scenes, as the plot has the title character entering parliament as the representative for Staines.

SOUTH-WEST LONDON

KEY
1. 102 Dalmatians (2000)
2. The Avengers (1998)
3. Ali G Indahouse (2002)
4. Genevieve (1953)
5. Seven Days to Noon (1950)
6. 28 Days Later (2002)

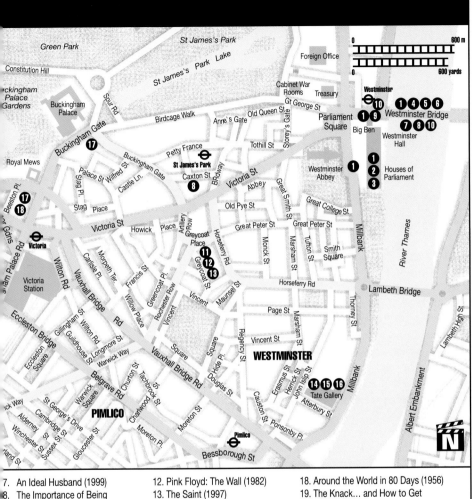

7. An Ideal Husband (1999)
8. The Importance of Being Earnest (2002)
9. The Thirty-Nine Steps (1978)
10. Defence of the Realm (1985)
11. Indiana Jones and the Last Crusade (1989)
12. Pink Floyd: The Wall (1982)
13. The Saint (1997)
14. Mission: Impossible (1996)
15. Bean (1997)
16. Love and Death on Long Island (1998)
17. Howards End (1992)
18. Around the World in 80 Days (1956)
19. The Knack… and How to Get It (1965)
20. The Fallen Idol (1948)
21. The Million Pound Note (1953)
22. The Crying Game (1992)
23. Four Weddings and a Funeral (1994)

The lighthearted British film **Genevieve** (1953), about two couples taking part in the annual vintage car race between London and Brighton, has a scene in which one of the cars traps its wheels in the old tramlines that once ran across Westminster Bridge. When the film was shot the tramlines had disappeared, so the actual filming took place in Lewisham, with backgrounds shot at Westminster.

Goldie (played by Olive Sloane) looks to escape explosion-threatened London in Seven Days to Noon *(1950).*

Just three years earlier, the science-fiction drama **Seven Days to Noon** (1950) was made by the producer/director partnership of identical twins John and Roy Boulting. The scenario was based around the threat of an atomic explosion in London, which causes a mass exodus from the city. In one scene, a lorry full of soldiers stops to pick up Goldie (Olive Sloane) on Westminster Bridge – with the tram tracks then still in place.

Roy Boulting recalled filming the scenes where London is evacuated. In an interview he said: 'For this – I think, chilling moment – we naturally chose areas of London normally swarming with people. Westminster Bridge, for example, Covent Garden, Piccadilly Circus, Regent's Park and the Zoo. I tell you, to achieve this was quite a job.' He added that not one frame was special effects, with virtually the entire film shot on location.

Seven Days to Noon is echoed – though with a different spin – in **28 Days Later** (2002), directed by Danny Boyle from a script by Alex Garland. (Boyle and Garland also worked together on the film of Garland's bestselling novel *The Beach*.) Shot entirely digitally, the film is about a man (Cillian Murphy) who wakes from a 28-day coma to find the world ravaged by a man-made virus. The film features images of a desolate London, including a deserted Westminster Bridge. Also cast in the film are Christopher Eccleston (as a soldier who may offer answers to the situation), Naomie Harris and Brendan Gleeson.

Westminster Bridge can also be seen as a backdrop in the 1999 film adaptation of Oscar Wilde's *An Ideal Husband*, starring Rupert Everett and Cate Blanchett. Another adaptation of one of Wilde's witty classics, **The Importance of Being Earnest** (2002), directed by Oliver Parker and starring Colin Firth, Rupert Everett,

Reese Witherspoon and Judi Dench, also used the area as a key period location. The location team had to recreate the Savoy Hotel of the early 20th century. St Ermine's Hotel in Caxton Street, Westminster agreed to have their ballroom transformed, and location manager .Christian McWilliams said, 'I've never known a hotel agree to a crew completely making over one of their rooms.' The management were so impressed by the make-over that they kept the room intact.

Robert Powell, as the heroic Richard Hannay, hangs from the hands of Big Ben in the climax to The Thirty-Nine Steps *(1978).*

The climax to **The Thirty-Nine Steps** (1978) is supposedly set on Big Ben at Westminster, with Richard Hannay (Robert Powell) dangling from the hands of the clock. Naturally enough, this was shot on a studio set. In **Defence of the Realm** (1985), directed by David Drury, one of key early scenes sees grizzled old hack Vernon Bayliss (Denholm Elliott) meeting with his contact Dennis Markham (Ian Bannen) under the shadow of Big Ben. They meet on Westminster Bridge with views of County Hall on the other side of the river behind them.

The Royal Horticultural Hall on Greycoat Street also occasionally features in films. In Alan Parker's **Pink Floyd: The Wall** (1982), the hall was used for a scene where Pink (Bob Geldof) takes charge of a neo-fascist rally. Meanwhile, in **Indiana Jones and the Last Crusade** (1989), directed by Steven Spielberg and starring Harrison Ford and Sean Connery, the hall became the interior of Berlin airport, and doubled as Berlin Templehof airport again in **The Saint** (1997), which starred Val Kilmer in the title role.

PIMLICO

The Tate Britain art gallery, located close to the river on Millbank, has played a part in several films over the years. In Brian De Palma's **Mission: Impossible** (1996), starring Tom Cruise, the Tate Britain was used to double as the entrance to an embassy in Prague; in the hit comedy **Bean** (1997), with Rowan Atkinson as the inept Mr Bean, the gallery's interiors are used for the London gallery he works for. The Tate Britain can also be seen in the gallery scenes of **Love and Death on Long Island** (1998), directed by Richard Kwietniowski and starring John Hurt.

VICTORIA

The St James Court Hotel in Buckingham Gate doubled as the exterior of the London home of Henry Wilcox (Anthony Hopkins) in **Howards End** (1992). Scenes were also shot in Victoria Square, north of Victoria Station. In the film, the home of the Schlegel sisters Margaret (Emma Thompson) and Helen (Helena Bonham Carter) is located in the quiet square, which can also be seen in scenes from the epic version of **Around the World in 80 Days** (1956). In Richard Lester's **The Knack… and How to Get It** (1965) naïve Nancy Jones (Rita Tushingham) arrives at Victoria Coach Station.

BELGRAVIA

The wealthy streets of Belgravia have played host to a number of film sets. In Carol Reed's thriller **The Fallen Idol** (1948), adapted from Graham Greene's short story *The Basement Room*, Ralph Richardson played a butler accused of murder, with young Bobby Henry as the ambassador's son who attempts to help him. The embassy is actually the headquarters of St John's Ambulance, located on Belgrave Square, while the streets where Bobby gets lost are Kinnerton Street and Belgrave Mews.

Belgravia is also the location for the lovely house at 47 Belgrave Square that is owned by rich London gambler Roderick Montpelier (Wilfred Hyde White) in the film **The Million Pound Note** (1953). As a joke, Montpelier gives a million-pound note to penniless American Henry Adams (Gregory Peck), who is told to keep it intact for a month, after which he can keep the money. The joke is turned on Montpelier as Adams finds he doesn't need to spend real money as the note gives him a wonderfully high credit rating.

The Crying Game (1992) used the Lowndes Arms, 37 Chesham Street for a scene involving Stephen Rea and Miranda Richardson, while nearby 100 Eaton Place was used for an attempted assassination scene.

Sloane Square
It is in Sloane Square, on the edge of Belgravia that Charles (Hugh Grant) reluctantly helps Carrie (Andie MacDowell) choose her wedding dress in **Four Weddings and a Funeral** (1994). The shop used was Albrissi at 1 Sloane Square.

LOCATION LONDON

ACTOR *Christopher Lee*

DATES *born 1922*

That mainstay of horror and fantasy films **Christopher Lee** was born at 51 Lower Belgrave Street, Belgravia on 27 May 1922, the son of Lieutenant Colonel Geoffrey Lee and Contessa Estelle Marie Carandini. After the Second World War he ventured into acting, making his first appearance in *Corridor of Mirrors* (1948). When Lee was cast as 'The Creature' in the Hammer horror film *The Curse of Frankenstein* (1957) he found his cinematic forte, and when he played the lead in *Dracula* (1958) his fame was sealed. Lee played The Prince of Darkness in several sequels, and starred in many other films made by Hammer Studios, including *The Hound of the Baskervilles* (1959) and *Rasputin the Mad Monk* (1965). Other films include *The Wicker Man* (1973) and *The Man with the Golden Gun* (1974). He has also had key roles in two of the biggest fantasy films of recent times, *The Lord of the Rings: Fellowship of the Ring* (2001) and *Star Wars: Episode II – Attack of the Clones* (2002).

KNIGHTSBRIDGE

Though the majority of Michael Powell and Emeric Pressburger's controversial (for its time) **The Life and Death of Colonel Blimp** (1943) was shot in a studio, the exterior of the London house of Blimp (a masterful performance by Roger Livesey) was actually 15 Ovington Square.

The department store Harrods, which is undoubtedly one of the area's most famous landmarks, appeared in **Mad Cows** (1999) with Harrods' boss Mohamed al-Fayed taking on a cameo role as a Harrods doorman. The film, based on Kathy Lette's best-selling novel, starred Anna Friel as an Australian single-mother tackling the English establishment. Harrods can also be seen in out-takes from the comedy **Bean** (1997), which has the disaster-prone title character (played as usual by Rowan Atkinson) driving a Mini car through the store.

The updated version of **The Parent Trap** (1998) shot in both London and the USA. Lindsay Lohan played twin sisters (Hayley Mills took the roles in the 1961 original) whose parents live in different countries. One shares a house with the mother, wedding dress designer Elizabeth James (Natasha Richardson), while the other twin lives with the father Nick (Dennis Quaid) a Californian vineyard owner. The London house scenes were shot at 23 Egerton Terrace, with other scenes shot at The Boltons, in nearby South Kensington.

SOUTH-WEST LONDON

KEY

1. The Life and Death of Colonel Blimp (1943)
2. Mad Cows (1999)
3. Bean (1997)
4. The Parent Trap (1998)
5. The Wings of the Dove (1997)
6. Genevieve (1953)
7. Spiceworld: The Movie (1997)
8. The Party's Over (1965)
9. B Monkey (1996)
10. The Servant (1963)
11. The Avengers (1998)
12. A Clockwork Orange (1971)
13. Sliding Doors (1998)
14. Absolute Beginners (1986)
15. Theatre of Blood (1973)
16. Maybe Baby (2000)
17. Around The World in Eighty Days (1956)
18. The Titfield Thunderbolt (1953)
19. Brassed Off (1996)
20. The Man Who Knew Too Much (1934 & 1956)
21. The X-Files: The Movie (1998)
22. Shine (1996)
23. The Thirty-Nine Steps (1978)
24. 101 Dalmatians (1996)
25. Loch Ness (1995)
26. One of Our Dinosaurs is Missing (1975)
27. Portrait of a Lady (1996)
28. Repulsion (1965)

Serpentine Gallery
Hyde Park
Royal Albert Hall
KNIGHTSBRIDGE
Kensington Rd
Knightsbridge
South Carriage Drive
Prince Consort Rd
Royal College of Music
Imperial College
Science Museum
Natural History Museum
Victoria & Albert Museum
Cromwell Rd
BROMPTON
Thurloe Place
Thurloe St
South Kensington
Old Brompton Rd
Onslow Square
Fulham Rd
SOUTH KENSINGTON
CHELSEA
King's Rd
Cheyne Walk
Chelsea Embankment
River Thames
Albert Bridge

0 300 m
0 300 yards

Hyde Park

In Iain Softley's lush adaptation of **The Wings of the Dove** (1997) – based on the Henry James novel – the scheming lovers Kate Croy (Helena Bonham Carter) and Merton Densher (Linus Roache) meet up with the innocent heiress Millie Theale (Alison Elliott) at the Serpentine Gallery in Hyde Park. The park can also be seen in a sequence from the charming comedy **Genevieve** (1953), starring Kay Kendall and Kenneth More, which is about participants in the London to Brighton classic car race.

Vintage cars gather in Hyde Park for the start of the London to Brighton car race in Genevieve *(1953).*

LOCATION LONDON

ACTOR *David Niven*

DATES *1910-1983*

Though many sources state that he was born in the Scottish town of Kirriemuir, in fact that elegant and witty leading man **David Niven** was born in March 1910 at Belgrave Mansions, Knightsbridge.

In his autobiographies, the most famous of which is *The Moon's a Balloon* (1972), Niven never fully reveals his origins, and it seems likely that his background was manufactured by the Hollywood publicity machine. After serving in the Army, Niven left for the USA, and following spells in New York and Atlantic City, he eventually drifted to Los Angeles where he found work as an extra. His innate charm and intelligence helped open doors and he found his way into a variety of films, developing in later years into a talented actor, and winning an Oscar for his performance in *Separate Tables* (1958). Other films in which Niven starred include *Wuthering Heights* (1939), *A Matter of Life and Death* (1945) and *The Guns of Navarone* (1961).

CHELSEA

The backbone of the affluent area of Chelsea is the King's Road, which came into its own as a fashionable shopping venue in the 1960s, and remains so today. In **Spiceworld: The Movie** (1997), we see the Spice Girls take a bus ride through London that takes them along the King's Road, while filming also took place at the Chelsea and Westminster Hospital on Fulham road.

A bizarre film entitled **The Party's Over** (1965) – a tale of bright young things in Chelsea (led by Oliver Reed) who link up with an American girl who ends up dead – was actually shot in 1963, but banned by the British censor until it was re-edited. After the re-edit, the director, Guy Hamilton, took his name off the film as he didn't see it as his work. The story delves into necrophilia, which was (unsurprisingly) the reason the censors got a little touchy about the film.

The little-seen romantic thriller **B Monkey** (1996), directed by Michael Radford, shot in and around Chelsea. Scenes were shot on the Albert Bridge, in Glebe Place and at the Michelin Building on Fulham Road. Sexy jewel thief Beatrice (Asia Argento) – aka B Monkey – wants to go straight, but the London underworld is against her. The attentions of a schoolteacher (Jared Leto) make things easier.

In **The Servant** (1963) James Fox starred as an ineffectual wealthy young man who is gradually manipulated and trapped in his own home by his manservant (Dirk Bogarde) and his manservant's sister (Sarah Miles). Directed by Joseph Losey from a script by Harold Pinter – who also has a small cameo role as 'Society Man' – this claustrophobic film caused something of an outrage when first released due to its homoerotic undertones. However, like so many contentious movies, it went on to be regarded as one of the best British films ever made. Fox's Georgian house was

actually 30 Royal Avenue in Chelsea. Bogarde – who also took over some of the directing chores while Losey was hospitalized for two weeks – recalled: 'There was no elaborate set; it was simply the house, an actual house in Chelsea, and Joe used the house as the metaphor all the way through.'

Joseph Losey's The Servant *(1963) shot in Royal Avenue, Chelsea.*

LOCATION LONDON

DIRECTOR *Joseph Losey*

DATES *1909-1984*

Director **Joseph Losey** was born in Wisconsin but moved to the UK after being branded a communist and being blacklisted in the US. He initially worked under several pseudonyms and later gained a reputation as a stylish director. His films include *The Servant* (1963), *Accident* (1967) and *The Go-Between* (1971). After shooting *The Servant* in Chelsea, he bought property in the area – 29 Royal Avenue – on the opposite side of the road from the house he had filmed in. He lived there until his death in 1984.

Parts of the big-budget fantasy adventure **The Avengers** (1998) also shot in Royal Avenue. The scenes of Emma Peel's (Uma Thurman) stylish flat were shot at the real-life home of architect Lord Richard Rogers at 45 Royal Avenue.

Albert Bridge and Cheyne Walk

In Stanley Kubrick's **A Clockwork Orange** (1971), scenes towards the end of the film were shot in Chelsea. Alex (Malcolm McDowell) has undergone 'gross aversion therapy' to help him mend his violent ways, and at Chelsea Embankment he comes across a tramp that he had attacked earlier in the story; under Albert Bridge a band of down-and-outs take their revenge on the now defenceless Alex.

Albert Bridge provides a great backdrop for many films, both day and night.

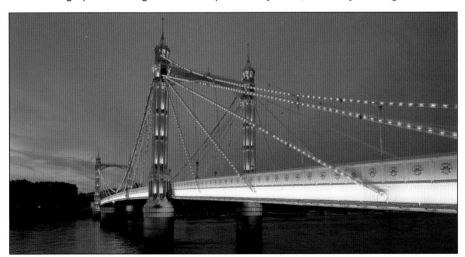

Albert Bridge can be seen in one of the closing scenes of the romantic comedy **Sliding Doors** (1998). Towards the end of the film Helen and James (Gwyneth Paltrow and John Hannah) reconcile on the bridge in the pouring rain. The bridge was also used as a backdrop for one of the musical numbers in Julien Temple's **Absolute Beginners** (1986). Based on Colin MacInnes' cult novel, the film was set in the late 1950s and starred Patsy Kensit and Eddie O'Connell. It was something of a failure in its attempt to make a British musical, but it remains interesting viewing. The Notting Hill and Soho sets were built at Shepperton Studios, but in one location shot Eddie O'Connell's Colin Young sings 'Have You Ever Had it Blue' (performed by Paul Weller and The Style Council) on the bridge.

It was at 8 Cheyne Walk, which overlooks Albert Bridge, that poor old Diana Dors was strangled – by Jack Hawkins of all people – in the witty horror film **Theatre of Blood** (1973). The film features a tour-de-force performance by Vincent Price as an actor who vows revenge on his critics. Albert Bridge is also seen in the title sequence of Ben Elton's **Maybe Baby** (2000).

Mike Todd's epic portmanteau film **Around the World in Eighty Days** (1956) shot scenes all around London for the early sequences, before Phileas Fogg (David Niven) and his man servant Passepartout (Cantinflas) head off on their global journey; a scene in which Passepartout cycles a pennyfarthing was shot on Upper Cheyne Row just north of the Albert Bridge.

SOUTH KENSINGTON

The endearing Ealing comedy **The Titfield Thunderbolt** (1953), directed by Charles Crichton, tells the story of the inhabitants of the fictional village of Titfield, who, finding their steam railway line under threat, join together to run things themselves. Though mostly shot near Bath, the film has one key London scene in which the villagers sneak the train, the *Titfield Thunderbolt*, from a local museum. This was filmed at the old Imperial Institute on Exhibition Road, Kensington, now the site of Imperial College.

Royal Albert Hall

The Royal Albert Hall is an oft-used location for film-makers, who like to use both the interior (for concert scenes) and the exterior, which provides a grandiose backdrop. The closing scenes of the superb British drama **Brassed Off** (1996), about the implications of pit closures on a northern town and the attempts to keep a colliery brass band going, were shot at the Albert Hall. The band, led by Pete Postlethwaite (and featuring Ewan McGregor and Tara Fitzgerald among its line-up), takes part in the finals of a national brass band competition at the Albert Hall. They win, though Postlethwaite then gives an impassioned speech about the

Villagers take the law into their own hands and reclaim their favoured steam train in the Ealing comedy The Titfield Thunderbolt *(1953).*

government and the state of the mining industry, handing back their trophy. The closing scene sees the band travelling around London on a double-decker bus.

Alfred Hitchcock shot the climax for both of his versions of **The Man Who Knew Too Much** (1934 and 1956) at the Albert Hall. His first film starred Leslie Banks and Edna Best, while the second version (in colour) starred James Stewart and Doris Day. In a rather different vein, the Albert Hall featured in the closing concert scenes of **Spiceworld: The Movie** (1997), directed by Bob Spiers and starring – who else? – the Spice Girls.

Even **The X-Files: The Movie** (1998), directed by Rob Bowman, made a visit to Kensington, though Mulder (David Duchovny) and Scully (Gillian Anderson) did not make the trip. In an early scene a character known as 'the well-manicured man' visits a conspiratorial group in London to discuss what to do about those pesky FBI agents. The meeting of the group is at Queen Alexandra's House, Kensington Gore, making good use of the Albert Hall in the background.

The Oscar-winning **Shine** (1996) told the story of troubled Australian pianist David Helfgott, who was played by Geoffrey Rush as the older Helfgott and Noah

Taylor as the younger. Scenes of Helfgott studying music in London were filmed at the Royal College of Music on Prince Consort Road, opposite the Albert Hall.

In **The Thirty-Nine Steps** (1978), the flat owned by Richard Hannay (Robert Powell) is actually at Albert Court, which sits alongside the Albert Hall.

South Kensington

Slight errors do crop up in the entertaining family film **101 Dalmatians** (1996), including a scene shot at Roger (Jeff Daniels) and Anita's (Joely Richardson) flat. Although the flat was supposed to be in South Kensington it somehow manages to have a view of Big Ben and the Thames that was clearly shot from south of the river.

Joely Richardson also appeared – this time alongside Ted Danson – in the endearing comedy **Loch Ness** (1995). An early scene was filmed at the Natural History Museum, though, obviously enough, the majority of the remaining locations were in Scotland. Party scenes from Sara Sugerman's comedy **Mad Cows** (1999) were also shot at the museum.

The Natural History Museum was used as a delightful location for the Disney family comedy **One of Our Dinosaurs is Missing** (1975), directed by Robert Stevenson. Derek Nimmo plays the spy Lord Southmere who has a stolen microfilm Lotus X and is being chased by Chinese spies. He stashes the film inside a large dinosaur at the Natural History Museum, and while there bumps into his former nanny Hettie (played by American veteran actress Helen Hayes). Before Southmere is captured he asks for Hettie's help, and before long Hettie, her nanny friends and several young charges are involved in the wacky spy plot as they seek to rescue Lord Southmere from the evil Chinese spy boss Hnup Wan (played with relish by Peter Ustinov). In other memorable scenes the stolen dinosaur skeleton is transported onto a lorry and driven through the foggy London streets.

The Victoria and Albert Museum appeared in Jane Campion's **Portrait of a Lady** (1996), which starred Nicole Kidman in a tasteful version of the Henry James novel.

In Roman Polanski's **Repulsion** (1965), the beauty salon in which repressed Belgian manicurist Carol Ledoux (Catherine Deneuve) works is at 31 Thurloe Place, while close by is the Hoop and Toy pub, where Colin (John Frazer) drinks with his buddies. He and Carol can also be seen heading off for fish and chips at Dino's, close to South Kensington tube station. Nasty deaths follow, but then this is a Polanski film so death should be expected.

WANDSWORTH

Stephen Frears' groundbreaking drama **My Beautiful Laundrette** (1985) not only revitalized the British film industry in the mid-1980s, but it also highlighted Daniel Day-Lewis as an acting talent to watch, particularly as it came out in the same year

Daniel Day Lewis and Gordon Warnecke in My Beautiful Laundrette *(1985).*

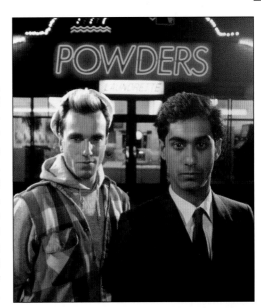

in which he played Cecil Vyse in *A Room with a View*. In *My Beautiful Laundrette* he was Johnny, a one-time racist who falls for Omar (Gordon Warnecke) whose dream is to establish a successful laundrette. The building used to film the laundrette was at 11 Wilcox Road, off the Wandsworth Road, while the newsagent shop featured heavily in the film is at 169–71 Wandsworth Road. The scene in which Omar is attacked was shot under the railway bridge that crosses Stewart's Road.

VAUXHALL

Situated on the south bank of the River Thames at Vauxhall Cross is the MI6 building, which, naturally enough, crops up in several films featuring super-spy James Bond.

The pre-credits sequence of **The World is Not Enough** (1999) features a memorable sequence in which a killer in a power boat out on the Thames shoots at Bond while he is in the MI6 building headquarters. In the film, Bond (Pierce Brosnan) leaps into the souped-up MI6 boat and launches

The James Bond film The World is Not Enough *(1999) featured a speedboat chase along the River Thames.*

SOUTH-WEST LONDON

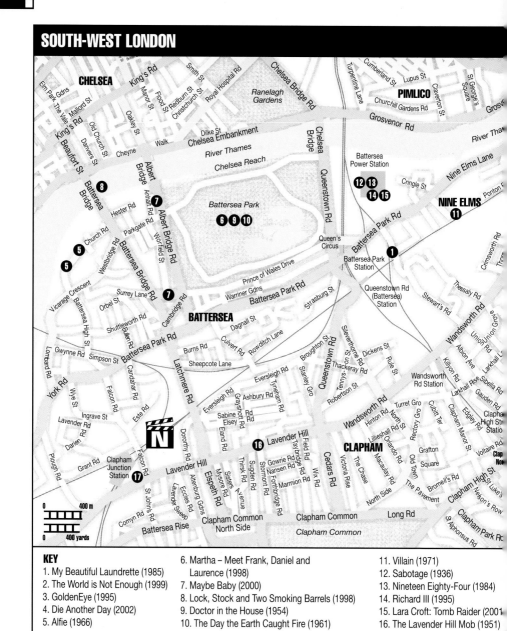

KEY

1. My Beautiful Laundrette (1985)
2. The World is Not Enough (1999)
3. GoldenEye (1995)
4. Die Another Day (2002)
5. Alfie (1966)

6. Martha – Meet Frank, Daniel and Laurence (1998)
7. Maybe Baby (2000)
8. Lock, Stock and Two Smoking Barrels (1998)
9. Doctor in the House (1954)
10. The Day the Earth Caught Fire (1961)

11. Villain (1971)
12. Sabotage (1936)
13. Nineteen Eighty-Four (1984)
14. Richard III (1995)
15. Lara Croft: Tomb Raider (2001)
16. The Lavender Hill Mob (1951)

himself onto the Thames and after the killer (Maria Grazia Cucinotta). The chase takes Bond along the river via the Royal Victoria Dock in Canning Town and Glengall Bridge at Milwall Inner Dock on the Isle of Dogs, before eventually arriving at Greenwich and the then-uncompleted Millennium Dome. The MI6 building can

SOUTH LAMBETH

STOCKWELL

BRIXTON

17. Up The Junction (1967)
18. Velvet Goldmine (1998)
19. South West 9 (2001)
20. Born Romantic (2000)
21. The Ploughman's Lunch (1983)

Joseph Fiennes and Monica Potter in the romantic comedy Martha – Meet Frank, Daniel and Laurence *(1998).*

also be spotted in the 1995 Bond film **GoldenEye**.

Look out for the MI6 building again in **Die Another Day** (2002), directed by Lee Tamahori, and with a cast including Halle Berry, Rosamund Pike, Judi Dench, John Cleese and Brosnan as Bond again. The film also includes Bond being shown his latest car by John Cleese in a fictional Vauxhall Cross tube station located beneath the spy headquarters, as well as featuring a memorable scene of bad guy Gustav Graves (Toby Stephens) making a parachute landing right in front of Buckingham Palace, closely watched by Bond.

The opening-credits scene of **Alfie** (1966) was filmed on Vauxhall Bridge, before moving on to locations all over London.

BATTERSEA

Many of the memorable scenes from the British comedy **Martha – Meet Frank, Daniel and Laurence** (1998) were filmed around Battersea. Directed by Nick Hamm, the film starred Monica Potter as the Martha of the title, a young American who decides to head off to Britain. She is romanced by three friends (Joseph Fiennes, Rufus Sewell and Tom Hollander), all unaware

that each is pursuing her. After spending her first night at a swish hotel (Blakes in Roland Gardens) she meets up with one of the boys in Battersea Park, sheltering in the bandstand and eating at the Battersea Park Café.

In Ben Elton's romantic comedy **Maybe Baby** (2000), the tasteful flat owned by the lead characters Sam and Lucy (Hugh Laurie and Joely Richardson) is at Waterside Point, Anhalt Road in Battersea. In the film's closing sequences, after much emotional angst and a trial separation, Lucy is living in a new flat, which was actually at Primrose Mansions, Prince of Wales Drive.

Meanwhile, the cliffhanging final scene of Guy Ritchie's gangster comedy **Lock, Stock and Two Smoking Barrels** (1998) was filmed on Battersea Bridge.

Key scenes from **Alfie** (1966) were filmed in Battersea. Scenes were shot of Julia Foster – who plays one of the many women Michael Caine's caddish cockney dallies with – lunching in Battersea Church Road, while at St Mary's, Battersea Parish Church, Alfie sees the christening of Foster's baby.

Earlier British films often make use of the old Battersea Funfair, which until the 1970s was located in Battersea Park. Films that featured the fair include **Doctor in the House** (1954) and **The Day the Earth Caught Fire** (1961).

The nearby Nine Elms area, home to London's vast wholesale fruit and vegetable market, was used as a backdrop for Michael Tuchner's British crime film **Villain** (1971), which was believed to have been inspired by the activities of the Kray twins. *Villain* starred Richard Burton as vicious gay East End gangster Vic Dakin, with a cast that included Ian McShane and Joss Ackland.

Battersea Power Station

The disused Battersea Power Station, off Battersea Park Road, can often be seen in movies as it offers an extraordinary backdrop and plenty of ground space for film-makers. Back in 1936, Alfred Hitchcock shot at the power station when it was still functioning. The opening scene of **Sabotage**, which starred Sylvia Sidney and Oscar Homolka, saw London plunged into darkness after someone disabled the power station. This striking London landmark also featured in Michael Radford's **Nineteen Eighty-Four** (1984) and can also be seen in the impressive 1995 adaptation of Shakespeare's **Richard III**.

For those with DVD players, Battersea Power Station can also be spotted in the out-takes section of **Lara Croft: Tomb Raider** (2001). In one of the scenes that didn't make the final film, Wilson (Leslie Philips), a friend of Lara's (Angelina Jolie), betrays her to conniving bad-guy Manfred Powell (Iain Glen), who murders Wilson rather nastily at Battersea Power Station.

Lavender Hill

Unsurprisingly for a film entitled **The Lavender Hill Mob** (1951), a substantial amount of filming for this classic Ealing comedy took place in Battersea's Lavender Hill area, although, the majority of the film was shot at Ealing Studios. The film starred Alec Guinness as a mild-mannered bank clerk who plots – with the aid of

An Alec Guinness comedy classic, The Lavender Hill Mob *(1951).*

his friend Stanley Holloway and two professional crooks – to steal gold bullion from a guarded van. Part of the plan involves leaving Guinness blindfolded and tied up in a warehouse, though he manages to stumble out and fall into the River Thames. The film was shot in a post-war London when working warehouses still lined the riverside. A delightful and much-loved caper-comedy, *The Lavender Hill Mob* is also worth watching to spot a young Audrey Hepburn, who plays Chiquita the cigarette girl in an opening scene.

LOCATION LONDON

ACTRESS *Margaret Rutherford*

DATES *1892-1972*

Margaret Rutherford was born at 15 Dornton Road, Balham, although she was only a few months old when her parents moved to India. Her parents' lives were blighted with tragedy; before Rutherford's birth, her father William Benn had murdered his father. He was committed to the asylum for the criminally insane at Broadmoor, changing his name to Rutherford when he was released seven years later. In India, young Margaret's mother Florence hanged herself, and her father returned to Broadmoor in 1904, where he remained until he died. Rutherford was brought up by her aunt in Wimbledon. After leaving school, she became a music teacher, later joining the Young Vic as a student. She was a wonderful and eccentric character actress, and her film roles include *Blithe Spirit* (1945), *The Importance of Being Earnest* (1952), *Passport to Pimlico* (1949) and the four films in which she played Agatha Christie's tweed-suited sleuth Miss Marple. She won an Oscar for her performance in *The VIPs* (1964).

LOCATION LONDON

ACTOR *Roger Moore*

DATES *born 1927*

As a child, **Roger Moore** – who later found fame playing heroes such as James Bond, Ivanhoe and Simon Templar – lived with his family in rented rooms at 4 Aldebert Terrace, situated between the South Lambeth Road and Clapham Road, later moving to nearby 16 Albert Square. After leaving school, Moore eventually found his way into the movies with a walk-on part in *Caesar and Cleopatra* (1946). Various small film roles followed, though fame actually came with television through starring roles in the series *Ivanhoe* (1957–58), *Maverick* (1960–61), *The Saint* (1967–69) and *The Persuaders* (1971–72). He went on to take over from Sean Connery as James Bond for seven films in the phenomenally popular series, beginning with *Live and Let Die* (1973) and ending with *A View to a Kill* (1985).

CLAPHAM

The film version of **Up The Junction** (1967), directed by Peter Collinson, starred Suzie Kendall as Polly, the uptown Chelsea girl who moves to live and work 'up the junction' in Clapham. Also in the cast were a young Dennis Waterman and Maureen Lipman. Nell Dunn's novel of the same name had previously been adapted for television by director Ken Loach, though his version was shot in a much grittier semi-documentary style.

BRIXTON

Brixton is an energetic and culturally diverse area of south-west London, something that can't help but be reflected in the films that shoot there.

Velvet Goldmine (1998), which was directed by Todd Haynes, was a fantastical look at the glam-rock era of the 1970s. It starred Ewan McGregor and Jonathan Rhys Meyers as characters who bear similarities to Iggy Pop and David Bowie. Most of the live rock-concert footage was filmed at the Brixton Academy at 211 Stockwell Road. McGregor asked if he could do his singing live. He recalled: 'Everyone sings with an American accent anyway so that's not hard and the vocals came from the thrashing around on stage, but it's definitely the most physical part

I've done. I can now say I've played the Brixton Academy!'

Brixton was the distinctive location for writer-director Richard Parry's debut film **South West 9** (2001), which followed five very different individuals – ranging from the obligatory drug-dealer to a white female Rastafarian – as they went about their business over a 24-hour period. Parry was formerly a news cameraman reporting from international hotspots, and for his feature debut he adopts a rather scattershot style of filming around Brixton, as his story ranges from clubs and riots to yuppies and would-be anarchists.

LOCATION LONDON

ACTOR *Claude Rains*

DATES *1889-1967*

The stylish star of such films as *Casablanca* (1943), *The Adventures of Robin Hood* (1938) and *Now, Voyager* (1942), **Claude Rains**, was born William Claude Rains at 26 Tregothnan Road, off Clapham Road in Stockwell. He started on the stage aged 11, and spent many years as a stage actor before switching to movies, making his debut at the ripe-old age of 44 in the title role of *The Invisible Man* (1933). Often cast as the villain, he went on to appear in some of Hollywood's most admired films, though is perhaps best remembered as Captain Renault walking off into the fog with Humphrey Bogart's Rick Blaine at the end of *Casablanca* (1942).

Toni Collette and Jonathan Rhys Meyers starred in Todd Haynes's glam-rock movie Velvet Goldmine (1998), which filmed several concert scenes in Brixton Academy.

'[*Born Romantic*] captures a truth about what it is like to be relatively young and living in a big city, so we had to show London how it is.'

MICHELE CAMARDA, PRODUCER
BORN ROMANTIC

In the comedy **Born Romantic** (2000), directed by David Kane, three couples find fun and romance at a London salsa club. The locations used were particularly authentic; the salsa club used was a real one in Brixton. 'While a lot of the locations are very striking and in new, trendy areas, the film doesn't glorify London,' explained the film's producer Michele Camarda.

In Richard Eyre's thoughtful drama **The Ploughman's Lunch** (1983), starring Jonathan Pryce, scenes were shot at Brixton tube station.

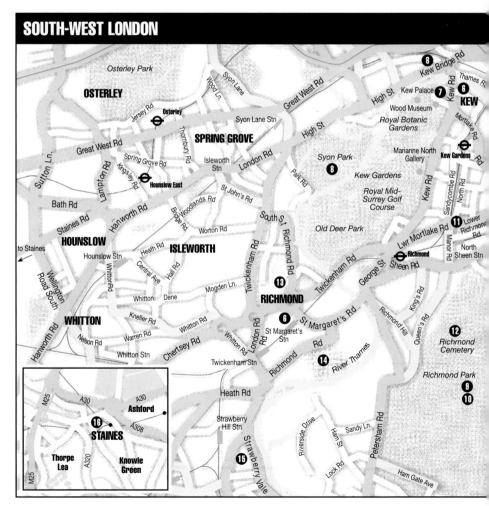

SOUTH-WEST LONDON

FULHAM

In Richard Donner's impressive horror film **The Omen** (1976) a seemingly batty priest (Patrick Troughton) makes the mistake of trying to tell US Ambassador Robert Thorn (played with gravitas by Gregory Peck) that his son Damien may not be quite what he seems; that is, he's the Antichrist. His mistake is costly as he ends up being run through by a lightning conductor from a church. This grisly scene was filmed on the Fulham side of Putney Bridge at All Saints' Church, which can be found on the north side of the river. Peck – unsurprisingly – is based at the American Embassy in Grosvenor Square, just below Oxford Street.

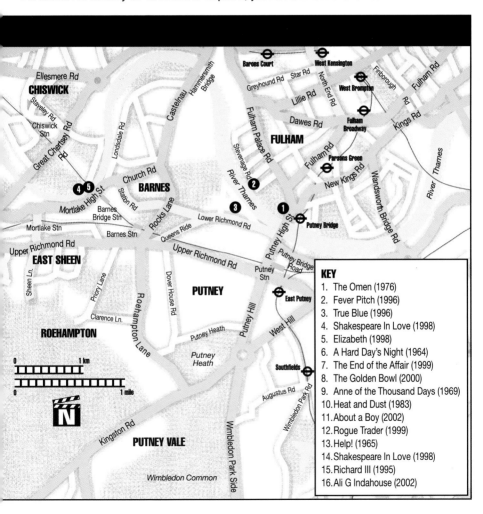

KEY
1. The Omen (1976)
2. Fever Pitch (1996)
3. True Blue (1996)
4. Shakespeare In Love (1998)
5. Elizabeth (1998)
6. A Hard Day's Night (1964)
7. The End of the Affair (1999)
8. The Golden Bowl (2000)
9. Anne of the Thousand Days (1969)
10. Heat and Dust (1983)
11. About a Boy (2002)
12. Rogue Trader (1999)
13. Help! (1965)
14. Shakespeare In Love (1998)
15. Richard III (1995)
16. Ali G Indahouse (2002)

Though much of the filming for the romantic comedy **Fever Pitch** (1996) took place at Arsenal in North London, some of the movie had to be shot elsewhere. When recreating the scenes set at Arsenal stadium in 1972 and 1989, the production team was unable to shoot inside Arsenal stadium itself due to the introduction of seating where once the fans would have stood on bare terraces. To stay faithful to the period, shooting took place at Craven Cottage, home of Fulham's football club, on the banks of the Thames.

PUTNEY

The true story of the 1987 Oxford and Cambridge Boat Race was recounted in Ferdinand Fairfax's **True Blue** (1996). The film tells the story of how top American oarsmen were recruited into the Oxford rowing team for the race. Featuring Johan Leysen, Dominic West and Dylan Baker, the film shot on the River Thames, making good use of the Putney Embankment.

BARNES

The pretty riverside area of Barnes does not crop up in films very often, though it was well used in **Shakespeare in Love** (1998), starring Joseph Fiennes as the playwright and Gwyneth Paltrow as his lover, Viola de Lesseps. The film was made at various locations around Britain, with much of the London of 1592 built from scratch at Shepperton Studios. However, key sequences were filmed on the River Thames at Barnes. In one notable scene a boat owner who is rowing Shakespeare across the river comments memorably in the style of a true London cabbie: 'I had that Christopher Marlowe in my boat once.'

The river near Barnes also served as a backdrop in another Oscar-nominated film set in the same period, this time **Elizabeth** (1998), directed by Shekhar Kapur and starring Cate Blanchett as the queen. Joseph Fiennes appears again in this film, playing Elizabeth's lover Robert Dudley.

KEW

The Beatles – well, at least Ringo – visited Kew when shooting the classic musical romp **A Hard Day's Night** (1964). Encouraged by Paul McCartney's mischievous Granddad (Wilfred Brambell), an unhappy Ringo takes a stroll prior to a concert along the Putney Towpath, close to Kew Bridge on the south side of the Thames. His mournful amble sees him ending up further west at the Turk's Head pub, Winchester Road in Twickenham.

   The End of the Affair (1999), Neil Jordan's adaptation of the Graham Greene novel set in the Second World War, starred Ralph Fiennes and Julianne Moore. It was primarily filmed in the south-coast town of Brighton, though the climactic scene, which sees a V1 rocket hitting a house, was shot at Kew Green. Another literary adaptation, James Ivory's elegant period film **The Golden Bowl** (2000), adapted

The atmospheric River Thames has featured in numerous films over the decades.

LOCATION LONDON

ACTOR *Ronald Colman*

DATES *1891-1958*

Screen idol **Ronald Colman** was born at Woodville, Sandycombe Road, Richmond (subsequently renamed and renumbered 7 Broomfield Road). Colman began work as a clerk acting with a local drama group in his spare time. After serving in the First World War, he decided to take up acting full-time, eventually getting small roles on stage and in silent films. He headed to New York where, after being spotted on stage by director Henry King, was cast opposite Lillian Gish in *The White Sister* (1923). Fame as a dashing romantic hero quickly followed, with Colman making an easy transition into sound from silent films. His films include *Beau Geste* (1926), and *A Double Life* (1947), for which he received an Oscar.

from the Henry James novel, shot at Kew Bridge Steam Museum and also made great use of Syon House in Brentford.

RICHMOND

The verdant splendour of Richmond Park was used for hunting scenes in the historical film **Anne of the Thousand Days** (1969). Henry VIII founded Richmond, and the film related the relationship between the king (Richard Burton) and Anne Boleyn (Genevieve Bujold). The park also featured briefly in James Ivory's **Heat and Dust** (1983), where it was used to film a dust storm, although the film was set in India.

Richmond was among the many London venues used by the production team of **About a Boy** (2002). The supermarket that Will (Hugh Grant) visits was Sainsbury's on Lower Richmond Road, while the shop where he buys baby gear was the Mothercare at Richmond Retail Park, Mortlake Road.

Richmond Cemetery was used for a scene in James Dearden's **Rogue Trader** (1999), the biopic of shamed trader Nick Leeson (Ewan McGregor), the man whose dealings brought about the collapse of Baring's Merchant Bank.

TWICKENHAM

With an active film studio based in nearby St Margaret's, the Twickenham area often crops up in films, though the fact that it is on the busy flight path to Heathrow airport does tend to hamper some period productions.

The wonderful scene in the second movie to feature The Beatles, **Help!** (1965), where the Fab Four enter the front doors of four terraced houses only to be in one massive house, was shot in the area. The houses that John, Paul, George and Ringo enter are actually 5, 7, 9 and 11 Ailsa Avenue, quite close to St Margaret's Road.

Marble Hill House in Twickenham provided a location for John Madden's Oscar-winning **Shakespeare in Love** (1998), while the Holbein Room of the Gothic revival Strawberry Hill House on Waldegrave Road can be seen in **Richard III** (1995), which stars Ian McKellen as Shakespeare's flawed king.

STAINES

Ali G Indahouse (2002) was the big screen adaptation of the cult comedy series on Britain's Channel 4. It saw Sacha Baron Cohen, as his shell-suited rapper Ali G, tackle problems in his 'manor'– Staines – as well as on a national scale.

The plot involces Ali G being set up as a parliamentary candidate for the south-west London commuter town in which he lives by the Deputy Prime Minister (Charles Dance) who hopes this will embarrass the Prime Minister. Ali is duly elected, but in turn discovers plans to build a new airport terminal in the area. To save the day, Ali recovers videotape that shows the Prime Minister in a compromising position with a woman of dubious nature.

The film was shot in and around London, and made – no surprise here – much use of Staines. Shooting also took place at Egham in Surrey, Isleworth in Middlesex and at Mentmore Towers in Buckinghamshire, which doubled as the Prime Minister's country house.

LOCATION LONDON

WRITER *Noël Coward*

DATES *1899-1973*

The noted wit and writer **Noël Coward** was born at 131 Waldegrave Road, Teddington to piano salesman Arthur Coward and his wife Violet. In 1908 he moved with his family to 70 Prince of Wales Mansions close to Battersea Park, and three years later, through his mother's intervention, made his first appearance on stage. He later began writing plays, and would become the highest paid writer of his generation. Many of his plays were adapted for the cinema, and in 1941 he wrote and produced the wartime film *In Which We Serve*. He co-wrote *Brief Encounter* (1945) and went on to appear in many films, including *Our Man in Havana* (1959) and *The Italian Job* (1969).

SOUTH-EAST LONDON

The south-east of London has long been favoured by film-makers who are looking for a period feel in their movies. At one time the warehouses of the docks and streets around Shad Thames and Bermondsey offered the perfect Dickensian backdrop, but the advent of expensive warehouse developments has put paid to that. Nevertheless, film-makers still make great use of areas such as Borough Market, an area that prides itself on its ability to work well with film crews. Greenwich is also a popular location, its grand Royal Naval College seeming to lend itself to just about any scenario, from doubling as the Pentagon in Washington, USA or Buckingham Palace to acting as the perfect backdrop of Elizabethan England.

The cobbled streets of Shad Thames have featured in both period movies and modern classics, such as *The French Lieutenant's Woman* (1981) and *Bridget Jones's Diary* (2001).

WATERLOO

Waterloo Station

Waterloo Station has often appeared in movies, with its distinctive front steps and large vaulted platform area. In the charming romantic classic **Bank Holiday** (1938), Margaret Lockwood played a nurse who plans a weekend in Brighton with her boyfriend but is drawn back to the hospital in which she works by a grieving widow. The film, directed by Carol Reed, has marvellous scenes of the holiday crowds gathering on the platforms of Waterloo Station as they head off to their resorts. Meanwhile, in **Waterloo Road** (1944), which starred Stewart Granger and John Mills, there is a chase scene across the tracks at the station.

The enjoyable wartime romp **Miss London Ltd**. (1943), the directorial debut of Val Guest, memorably opens with singing train announcers at Waterloo Station as various uniformed folk get on and off the trains. The opening scene also sees the arrival of Terry Arden (played with charm by Evelyn Dall) at the station, as she heads down the front steps of Waterloo to pick up a cab. She arrives in London to co-run a rundown escort agency with Arthur Bowman (Arthur Askey).

Waterloo Bridge (1931), directed by James Whale, told the story of two lovers who fall in love in London, though the film was shot in Hollywood. The 1940 remake (with the same title) eclipsed, rather unfairly, the original. Directed by Mervyn LeRoy, it starred Vivien Leigh and Robert Taylor as the lovers who meet on the bridge. This time the film shot actually on Waterloo Bridge, as well as at Waterloo Station, the South Bank and Hoxton Square.

Nicholas Nickleby (2002), directed and adapted from the Charles Dickens novel by Douglas McGrath, shot in both Yorkshire and London. The London locations included the Old Vic theatre, behind Waterloo Station on The Cut. The film stars Charlie Hunnam as the title character, and also includes Jamie Bell as Smike, Jim Broadbent as evil Wackford Squeers and Anne Hathaway as Madeline Bray.

A little further east along the river is the former Bankside power station, now the home of the Tate Modern art gallery. Before its refurbishment the power station was used as a location for Danny Cannon's comic-book adaptation **Judge Dredd** (1995), with Sylvester Stallone as the no-nonsense futuristic cop.

Holidaymakers at Waterloo Station in Bank Holiday *(1938).*

SOUTH-EAST LONDON

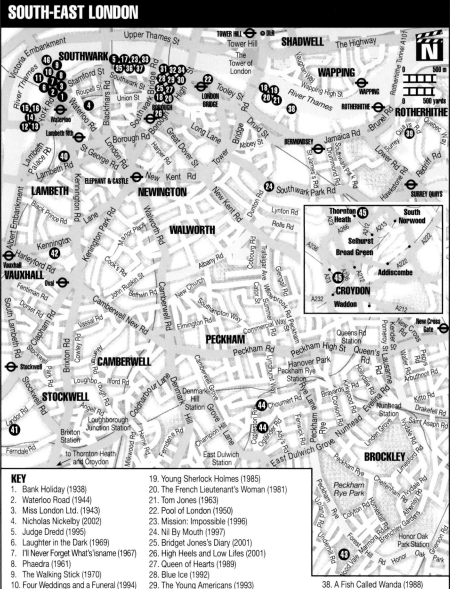

KEY
1. Bank Holiday (1938)
2. Waterloo Road (1944)
3. Miss London Ltd. (1943)
4. Nicholas Nickelby (2002)
5. Judge Dredd (1995)
6. Laughter in the Dark (1969)
7. I'll Never Forget What's'isname (1967)
8. Phaedra (1961)
9. The Walking Stick (1970)
10. Four Weddings and a Funeral (1994)
11. Truly Madly Deeply (1990)
12. The Mudlark (1950)
13. Frenzy (1972)
14. Scandal (1988)
15. Angels and Insects (1995)
16. Velvet Goldmine (1998)
17. Hue and Cry (1947)
18. The Elephant Man (1980)
19. Young Sherlock Holmes (1985)
20. The French Lieutenant's Woman (1981)
21. Tom Jones (1963)
22. Pool of London (1950)
23. Mission: Impossible (1996)
24. Nil By Mouth (1997)
25. Bridget Jones's Diary (2001)
26. High Heels and Low Lifes (2001)
27. Queen of Hearts (1989)
28. Blue Ice (1992)
29. The Young Americans (1993)
30. 101 Dalmatians (1996)
31. Wilde (1997)
32. Mojo (1997)
33. Keep the Aspidistra Flying (1998)
34. Entrapment (1999)
35. Lock, Stock and Two Smoking Barrels (1998)
36. Howards End (1992)
37. Johnny English (2002)
38. A Fish Called Wanda (1988)
39. Tomorrow Never Dies (1997)
40. Passport to Pimlico (1949)
41. Death Wish III (1985)
42. Spider (2002)
43. Entertaining Mr Sloane (1969)
44. Last Orders (2001)
45. Prick Up Your Ears (1987)
46. Waterloo Bridge (1931)

County Hall on the South Bank can be seen in many films from all eras.

South Bank Centre

Close to Waterloo Station, edging the river, is the South Bank Centre, an important arts complex that comprises the National Theatre, Royal Festival Hall, Hayward Gallery and the British Film Institute's National Film Theatre (NFT) and Imax Cinema. The NFT, which celebrated its 50th anniversary in 2002 and is generally regarded as the largest cinemathèque in the world, screens a wide range of film material from around the globe and has a dedicated membership of those who love all things cinematic. The NFT also plays host to many on-stage interviews with major actors, directors, screenwriters and technicians from all over the world.

The NFT can also be observed as a movie location itself on several occasions. In Tony Richardson's **Laughter in the Dark** (1969), Nicol Williamson enters the Curzon Mayfair cinema but finds himself in the NFT auditorium and is met by an ice-cream seller (please note, the NFT does not sell ice-cream!). The scenes actually had to be shot twice as Richard Burton was originally cast in the role but was replaced by Williamson. In Michael Winner's **I'll Never Forget What's'isname** (1967), cinema legend Orson Welles is seen attending an advertising awards ceremony staged at the NFT where Oliver Reed's character picks up a top prize. In **Phaedra** (1961), Anthony Perkins and Melina Mercouri meet up outside the NFT, while in **The Walking Stick** (1970) David Hemmings and Samantha Eggar pop in to see a film. More recently, in **Four Weddings and a Funeral** (1994) Charles (Hugh Grant) meets his mute brother David (David Bower) outside the NFT entrance and introduces him to Carrie (Andie McDowell), the woman he loves. Charles briefly goes into the cinema, but soon rushes out after Carrie and follows her along the river, explaining, rather amusingly in the words of a Partridge Family song, that he loves her.

Scenes from writer-director Anthony Minghella's romantic comedy **Truly Madly Deeply** (1990) made great use of London locations, although the majority of the film was shot in Bristol. In a charming scene filmed in front of the Royal Festival Hall, Nina (Juliet Stevenson) hops along the Thames Path while recounting her life story to prospective lover Mark (Michael Maloney). The film also starred Alan Rickman as Nina's late partner; Minghella went on to direct *The English Patient* (1996).

County Hall

Adjacent to the Royal Festival Hall and next to Westminster Bridge is County Hall, once the seat of the Greater London Council and now home to a hotel, aquarium and apartments.

In **The Mudlark** (1950), Big Ben and the Houses of Parliament can be seen in the background as Queen Victoria (Irene Dunne) is driven through the London streets, though this scene was actually filmed on the walkway in front of County Hall. In the opening shots of Alfred Hitchcock's **Frenzy** (1972) we see a woman's body washed up outside County Hall as a politician talks to a barely listening crowd – you can spot Hitchcock among the listeners.

County Hall can also be seen in the film **Scandal** (1988), starring Joanne Whalley and Bridget Fonda, and in the period drama **Angels and Insects** (1995), starring Mark Rylance and Patsy Kensit. In the glam-rock film **Velvet Goldmine** (1998), the title sequence shows youngsters in flares and stacked shoes running along the path on the south of the Thames, with glimpses of Big Ben in the background.

SOUTHWARK

The fine Ealing comedy (and the first of the genre) **Hue and Cry** (1947) made great use of bombed out areas of London. The film stars Alastair Sim who teams up with a group of East End youngsters (led by Harry Fowler) to thwart the fur-smuggling racket of a gang of crooks. The climax comes when the kids ambush the thieves in 'The Battle of Ballard's Wharf' which was shot at a bomb site at the southern end of Southwark

The final fight scene of the first Ealing comedy, Hue and Cry *(1947), shot close to Southwark Bridge.*

David Lynch's The Elephant Man *(1980), which starred John Hurt and Anthony Hopkins, shot in a variety of locations around London, including Shad Thames.*

Bridge, close to Bankside and Park Street. *Hue and Cry* offers an evocative look at post-war London.

Shad Thames, on the south bank of the Thames close to London Bridge, often features in films. The opening scenes of David Lynch's **The Elephant Man** (1980) used the cobbled streets of Shad Thames to recreate the streets of Victorian London, as did Barry Levinson's **Young Sherlock Holmes** (1985). *Young Sherlock Holmes* starred Nicholas Rowe as Sherlock and Alan Cox as a young Watson, who meet as children and solve a series of mysteries at school before heading to London to save Elizabeth (Sophie Ward), the obligatory damsel in distress. The area was also used as a backdrop in **The French Lieutenant's Woman** (1981) and Tony Richardson's **Tom Jones** (1963), which had Albert Finney in the title role and featured Susannah York.

The crime drama **Pool of London** (1950), directed by Basil Dearden, was set largely in the area around Tooley Street, in the days when the area was home to warehouses and shipping rather than fashionable living spaces. The film starred Earl Cameron and Susan Shaw and focuses on a tale about smuggling; it is notable as one of the first British films to feature a mixed-race romance.

At the close of **Mission: Impossible** (1996), directed by Brian De Palma, the pub where Tom Cruise and Ving Rhames meet up for a refreshing post-mission pint is actually the Anchor Tavern on Bankside, close to Southwark Bridge.

In the gritty urban drama **Nil By Mouth** (1997), director Gary Oldman used the local Wimpy Bar on Southwark Park Road in certain scenes.

THE BOROUGH

The streets around Borough Market, close to London Bridge, must count among London's most frequently used locations. It is particularly popular with film-makers who are trying to recreate historical London. Just as importantly, the community works well with film-makers and seems very much at ease with the broad range of movies that have been shot in the area. Borough Market was threatened with demolition a few years ago, but has, thankfully, weathered that crisis to establish itself as a prime London shooting venue.

One of the key locations for the comedy **Bridget Jones's Diary** (2001) was the Globe Tavern in Borough (where the real-life Great Train Robbery was planned in the 1960s). The pub provided the exterior to the upstairs flat in which Bridget (Renée Zellweger) alternately mourns lost love, writes her diary and cooks a

Renee Zellweger and Colin Firth caught in the snow in Bridget Jones's Diary *(2001).*

The streets around The Market Porter pub opposite Borough Market are extremely popular with film directors.

spectacularly awful meal. In the comedy **High Heels and Low Lifes** (2001), scenes in the hospital emergency department where Shannon (Minnie Driver) works were filmed in an old hospital in Borough.

The lighthearted caper **Entrapment** (1999) has a scene in which jewel thief Mac (Sean Connery) tests the loyalty of Virginia (Catherine Zeta Jones) by asking her to procure a vital roll of film from the owner of an antiques shop in Borough Market. A subsequent brawl sees the pair speeding through the market, with the bad guy blasting away at them with a pistol. Filming also took place at the Petit Robert Restaurant in Borough Market and at Limehouse Tunnel, further east.

Guy Ritchie's snappy crime film **Lock, Stock and Two Smoking Barrels** (1998) located the gang's hideout at 15 Park Street, opposite Borough Market. The building occupied by the gang's rival, Dog (Frank Harper), is next door – as in the film – at 13 Park Street. In **Howards End** (1992) the house where the impoverished Leonard Bast (Samuel West) lived was also on Park Street. The area was also used in the spy spoof **Johnny English** (2002), which stars Rowan Atkinson as a bumbling spy.

Other films that shot around Borough Market include **The Elephant Man** (1980), **The French Lieutenant's Woman** (1981), **Queen of Hearts** (1989), **Blue Ice** (1992), **The Young Americans** (1993), **101 Dalmatians** (1996), **Wilde** (1997) and **Mojo** (1997). The 1998 film **Keep the Aspidistra Flying** (based on the novel by George Orwell) also used the area, filming at the Borough Cafe on Park Street, which was converted into a butcher's shop for purposes of shooting.

BERMONDSEY

With their spectacular views over the River Thames and Tower Bridge, the expensive and fashionable apartments in renovated warehouses on the south side of the river make great locations. In the comedy **A Fish Called Wanda** (1988), directed by Charles Crichton, John Cleese played a barrister named Archie Leach (an in-joke as that was the real name of legendary actor Cary Grant) who falls for a seductive thief, Wanda, played by Jamie Lee Curtis.

In one scene, Archie borrows a riverside apartment for an assignation with Wanda – actually in New Concordia Wharf, Bermondsey Wall West – though his romantic plans are ruined by the arrival of her demented lover, Otto (played with Oscar-winning gusto by Kevin Kline), who proceeds to dangle Archie out of a window. This scene, though, was shot just downriver at the then undeveloped Reed's Wharf.

ROTHERHITHE

In the James Bond film **Tomorrow Never Dies** (1997), directed by Roger Spottiswoode, 007 (Pierce Brosnan) goes head-to-head with evil media mogul Elliot Carver (Jonathan Pryce). In one sequence he has to break into Carver's German printing works. These scenes were actually shot at two London print works – at the Harmsworth Quays Printers on Surrey Quays Road (which prints the London *Evening Standard*) and at Westferry Printers, 235 Westferry Road (which prints the *Daily Telegraph*).

LOCATION LONDON

ACTOR *Leslie Howard*

DATES *1893-1943*

The elegant British actor **Leslie Howard** – born Leslie Howard Steiner – was born at 31 Westbourne Road, Forest Hill (though the house has since been demolished). After serving in the First World War he started acting on stage in the UK and the US, making his film debut in *Outward Bound* (1930). Often cast as a gentle romantic lead, his films include *The Scarlet Pimpernel* (1935), *Pygmalion* (1938) and *Gone With the Wind* (1939).

LAMBETH

Despite its title, the whimsical comedy **Passport to Pimlico** (1949) was actually filmed across the river in Lambeth. Set shortly after the Second World War, the premise has the local residents of Pimlico finding an ancient document in a bomb crater that cedes the area to the Duke of Burgundy. Pimlico then declares itself an independent state in the heart of London as a way of avoiding post-war rationing, and sets up borders and trade agreements with other Londoners. After the government takes action against the Pimlico residents (or Burgundians as they style themselves) they even dig down and stop tube trains running under the streets and start asking for passports! Filming took place in Lambeth's bomb-damaged Hercules Road, where the film crew built houses and recreated destroyed buildings. Directed by Henry Cornelius, *Passport to Pimlico* had a wonderful cast with some of Britain's greatest character actors, including Stanley Holloway, Hermione Baddeley and Margaret Rutherford.

In Michael Winner's **Death Wish III** (1985), which was headlined by Charles Bronson as a vigilante cop, Lambeth Hospital stood in for the Bronx in New York.

The comedy classic Passport to Pimlico *(1949) actually shot in Lambeth; here, a helicopter hovers above the shooting location.*

KENNINGTON

Ralph Fiennes, star of *Schindler's List* (1993) and *The English Patient* (1996), starred in David Cronenberg's **Spider** (2002), a disturbing tale of a man who returns to the London locations that torment him after spending most of his life in a mental institution. Lynn Redgrave plays the formidable Mrs Wilkinson, who runs the seedy boarding house Spider (Fiennes) stays in. The exterior of Mrs Wilkinson's boarding house was shot in Kennington, south of the River Thames. 'We had to make it look as if Mrs Wilkinson's had a large central staircase and large rooms rather than being a tenement block, so we altered it a bit,' explained production designer Andrew Sanders. Spider's childhood haunts were represented by the gasworks at the Oval. Filming also took place at St Pancras Station and in Acton, Haringey and Deptford.

Ralph Fiennes said of the film: 'The London that Spider sees is his own quite strange take on things. He's been in an institution for most of his life – since he's been a boy of ten. In that time I think what he's remembered has become embellished and expanded by using his imagination. And it's all rooted in something terrible he's done. I think, in order to not face that, he's had to create this other unhappy childhood to protect himself. He is the victim of something appalling that was done to his mother, but it's not what Spider's created in his memory. He's trying to repress something horrific.'

Michael Caine (born Maurice Joseph Micklewhite) was born in March 1933, and as a youngster his family lived in a flat at 14 Urlwin Street, off Camberwell Road. He was evacuated from London during the Second World War, and on the family's return to London, Urlwin Street had been bomb-damaged, so they settled in a prefab in Marshall Gardens (now redeveloped) at Elephant and Castle, where they stayed for 18 years.

Caine stumbled into acting, and after completing his two years National Service, eventually found his way into theatre and cinema. His big break came with a key role in *Zulu* (1964) and led directly to other similarly anti-heroic, laconic leading roles in *The Ipcress File* (1965) and *Alfie* (1966), the film that secured his stardom. Caine's subsequent films include *Get Carter* (1971), *The Man Who Would be King* (1976), *California Suite* (1983), *Hannah and Her Sisters* (1985, for which he received an Oscar) and *The Cider House Rules* (1999, for which he was awarded his second Academy Award).

LOCATION LONDON

ACTOR *Charlie Chaplin*

DATES *1889-1977*

Sir Charles Spencer Chaplin, was born on Tuesday April 16, 1889 in East Street, Walworth, though not long after his family moved to West Square, Kennington, where his parents performed at nearby pubs in Kennington Road. In 1895, Charlie's mother Hannah (now separated from her husband Charlie Snr) became ill, and Charlie was taken first by relations and then went into care at the Lambeth Workhouse on Renfrew Road. In 1898, Charlie and his brother Sydney returned to their mother at 10 Farmer's Road (now renamed Kennington Park Gardens), and over the next few years they stayed with either their mother or father in a series of lodgings in the area. Charlie and Sydney once rented a flat at 15 Glenshaw Mansions, Brixton Road. When he turned 14, Charlie registered with Blackmore's Theatrical Agency at Bedford Street, Strand, and after two years touring with a stage production of *Sherlock Holmes*, joined Fred Karno's group of comedians in 1907.

Charlie toured France and the US with Karno's troupe, and in 1913 was spotted in the US and joined Mack Sennett at the Keystone Cop Company. The rest is history.

CAMBERWELL

Key scenes from the black comedy **Entertaining Mr Sloane** (1969), directed by Douglas Hickox and based on Joe Orton's play, were shot in Camberwell Old Cemetery at Honor Oak. In the film, a sister and brother (the inspired casting of Beryl Reid and Harry Andrews) compete for the sexual favours of a muscle-bound stud, Mr Sloane (Peter McEnery). The historic lodge where Reid tries to seduce McEnery is actually a Victorian house at the entrance to the cemetery on Forest Hill Road.

PECKHAM

Scenes from Fred Schepisi's sombre yet superb drama **Last Orders** (2001) shot in Peckham, using a disused warehouse in the area as a temporary studio. The film starred a group of Britain's finest actors: Michael Caine, Tom Courtenay, David

Hemmings, Bob Hoskins, Ray Winstone and Helen Mirren. Schepisi also shot extensively in neighbouring East Dulwich, recreating a butcher's shop and an undertakers on Bellenden Road, and using the nearby Wishing Well pub for all of the pub scenes. The film also shot in Bermondsey, Smithfield Market, Margate and Canterbury.

'Four hundred yards down the road from where we're sitting here in Peckham, is Wilson's Grammar School, the school I attended – I've gone full circle... from Hollywood, the bright lights, I'm back in Peckham after 40 years in the movies. It is funny.'

ACTOR MICHAEL CAINE, WHILE SHOOTING *LAST ORDERS*

CROYDON

Directed by Stephen Frears, **Prick Up Your Ears** (1987) told the life-story of playwright Joe Orton (Gary Oldman), who was murdered by his lover Kenneth Halliwell (Alfred Molina). In reality, the flat they shared was in Noel Road, Islington, though for purposes of shooting the film-makers used a house in Croydon. Meanwhile, nearby Thornton Heath doubled as Orton's childhood home of Leicester.

LOCATION LONDON

DIRECTOR *David Lean*

DATES *1908-1991*

Sir David Lean, one of the world's greatest film directors, was born at 38 Blenheim Crescent, South Croydon, to Quaker parents Frank Lean and Helena Tangye. Not long after his birth, though, the family moved to the village of Mertsham, near Reigate in Surrey. However, unable to educate David at the local Church of England school, the family returned to Croydon in 1915 and settled into Wareham Mount at 3 Wareham Road.

Lean started work in the film business as a general 'gofer' at Gaumont British's Lime Grove Studios in Shepherd's Bush, working in various departments before becoming an editor. He took his chance to direct when asked by Noël Coward to handle the action scenes in *In Which We Serve* (1942). He never looked back and went on to make some of the UK's greatest films, including *Brief Encounter* (1946), *Great Expectations* (1946), *Oliver Twist* (1948), *The Bridge on the River Kwai* (1957), *Lawrence of Arabia* (1962) and *Dr Zhivago* (1970).

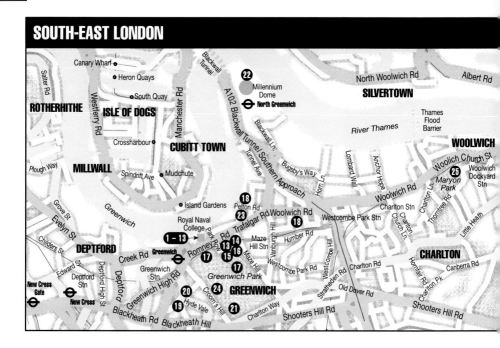

GREENWICH

The exquisite Royal Naval College, on the south side of the River Thames at Greenwich, regularly crops up in movies, with its elegant façade able to double for many locations, both historic and contemporary. In the action thriller **Patriot Games** (1992), directed by Philip Noyce, Harrison Ford's CIA analyst Jack Ryan visits a naval college to give a lecture. As he walks away from the building to meet up with his family he interrupts an attempted IRA splinter-group assassination of Lord Holmes (James Fox). The Royal Naval College doubles both as Buckingham Palace (for scenes of Lord Holmes's car leaving the building) and as the venue for Ford's academy lecture.

The romantic wartime drama **Charlotte Gray** (2001), directed by Gillian Armstrong and based on the best-selling novel by Sebastian Faulks, was shot largely in France, though certain key scenes were filmed in Scotland and London. Cate Blanchett starred in the title role as a young Scottish woman who comes to London to help in the war effort and finds herself becoming a spy in France. Early in the film she meets a government official (James Fleet) on the train for Scotland and is invited to a book launch. The venue for the launch is the fictional Southerby Square, which is in reality the courtyard of the Royal Naval College.

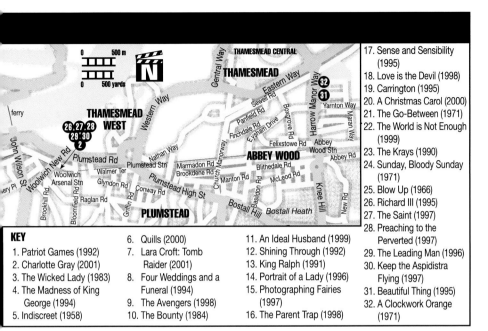

KEY
1. Patriot Games (1992)
2. Charlotte Gray (2001)
3. The Wicked Lady (1983)
4. The Madness of King George (1994)
5. Indiscreet (1958)
6. Quills (2000)
7. Lara Croft: Tomb Raider (2001)
8. Four Weddings and a Funeral (1994)
9. The Avengers (1998)
10. The Bounty (1984)
11. An Ideal Husband (1999)
12. Shining Through (1992)
13. King Ralph (1991)
14. Portrait of a Lady (1996)
15. Photographing Fairies (1997)
16. The Parent Trap (1998)
17. Sense and Sensibility (1995)
18. Love is the Devil (1998)
19. Carrington (1995)
20. A Christmas Carol (2000)
21. The Go-Between (1971)
22. The World is Not Enough (1999)
23. The Krays (1990)
24. Sunday, Bloody Sunday (1971)
25. Blow Up (1966)
26. Richard III (1995)
27. The Saint (1997)
28. Preaching to the Perverted (1997)
29. The Leading Man (1996)
30. Keep the Aspidistra Flying (1997)
31. Beautiful Thing (1995)
32. A Clockwork Orange (1971)

In Michael Winner's re-make of the classic Gainsborough melodrama **The Wicked Lady** (1983), which starred Faye Dunaway and Alan Bates, the scene in which Lady Skelton (Dunaway) meets King Charles II at The Duke's Theatre was actually shot in the Painted Hall of the Royal Naval College. The Painted Hall also provided the location for the scene in which the royal family attends a hand-bell concert in **The Madness of King George** (1994), starring Nigel Hawthorne as the ailing monarch; for the lodgings of the Prince of Wales (who was played with venom by Rupert Everett) they made use of another part of the college.

The venue can also be seen in the dance sequence between Cary Grant and Ingrid Bergman in Stanley Donen's **Indiscreet** (1958), and in Philip Kaufman's **Quills** (2000), an engaging drama about the Marquis de Sade that starred Geoffrey Rush, Michael Caine and Kate Winslet.

The Painted Hall also doubled as the Venetian headquarters of the Illuminati, the sinister organization plotting to take over the world, in the all-action **Lara Croft: Tomb Raider** (2001), which starred Angelina Jolie in the title role. In the film, directed by Simon West, she has a minor showdown with the chief villain Manfred Powell (Iain Glen) in the hall, ably throwing a knife into the symbol of the Illuminati.

Wedding number two in **Four Weddings and a Funeral** (1994) was shot in the chapel of the Royal Naval College. This is the wedding where Rowan Atkinson's bumbling clergyman delivered his hilarious 'holy goat' gaffe while trying to marry the happy couple.

More of the Royal Naval College can be seen in scenes from **The Avengers** (1998); the college doubled as the fictional World Council headquarters, which receives a threatening message from a mad weather fiend (Sean Connery). It can also be viewed in Roger Donaldson's **The Bounty** (1984) with Mel Gibson and Anthony Hopkins; **An Ideal Husband** (1999), starring Rupert Everett and Cate Blanchett; **Shining Through** (1992), in which the college stands in for the Pentagon, and **King Ralph** (1991), with John Goodman as an American who inherits the British throne.

King Ralph also filmed at nearby Park Row, which runs alongside Greenwich Royal Palace. Park Row can also be seen in Jane Campion's **Portrait of a Lady** (1996), featuring Nicole Kidman; **Photographing Fairies** (1997), directed by Nick Willing and starring Ben Kingsley and **The Parent Trap** (1998), directed by Nancy Myers and starring Natasha Richardson and Dennis Quaid.

The London street scenes in Ang Lee's **Sense and Sensibility** (1995) were shot at the restored Queen's House in Greenwich and nearby Greenwich Park. The acclaimed drama **Love is the Devil** (1998), directed by John Maybury, about the relationship between artist Francis Bacon (Derek Jacobi) and reformed thief George Dyer (Daniel Craig), shot at the Royal Standard pub and the Pickwick pub, both in Greenwich.

Christopher Hampton's drama **Carrington** (1995), starring Emma Thompson and Jonathan Pryce, shot scenes in Gloucester Circus, located behind Royal Hill close to Greenwich Park. The area was also used for the early live-action scenes in the largely animated version of **A Christmas Carol** (2000), which featured Simon Callow as Charles Dickens.

Nearby Greenwich Park features in Joseph Losey's period drama **The Go-Between** (1971), a lovely adaptation of L.P. Hartley's Edwardian romance, which was largely shot on location in Norfolk.

The opening action-packed pre-credits sequence of the James Bond film **The World is Not Enough** (1999) climaxes at the Millennium Dome at Greenwich. In the

The Royal Naval College in Greenwich is a perfect period setting.

scene, Bond (Pierce Brosnan) has chased a machine-gun wielding killer (Maria Grazia Cucinotta) along the River Thames to the Dome. The killer attempts to escape in a hot-air balloon, with Bond clinging to a rope dangling from the basket; when she blows up the balloon, Bond drops onto the side of the controversial building.

The East End of the 1930s was recreated in Caradoc Street, Greenwich with a two-up, two-down house used to double as the childhood home of gangsters Ronnie and Reggie Kray for the film **The Krays** (1990),

LOCATION LONDON

ACTOR *Bob Hope*

DATES *born 1903*

The much-loved comedian **Bob Hope**, though very much an American institution, was actually born in Britain. He was born Leslie Towns Hope on 29 May 1903 at 44 Craigton Road, Eltham, to stonemason Harry Hope and his wife Avis. To find work the family emigrated to Cleveland, Ohio, in 1908, with young Leslie trying his hand at many jobs before settling as a vaudeville comic and dancer. Hope is probably best known for the series of *Road To...* movies in which he starred with crooner Bing Crosby (who Hope had known and sparred with since they met on a radio show in the 1930s) and actress Dorothy Lamour. The first in the series, *Road to Singapore* (1940), was a massive hit, resulting in a further six films. Other Hope classics include *The Cat and the Canary* (1939), *The Ghost Breakers* (1940) and *The Paleface* (1948)

directed by Peter Medak. Pop-star brothers Gary and Martin Kemp were cast as the mobsters, who, in their heyday, were fearsome figures in the London underworld. The Krays were sentenced to life imprisonment in 1969 for murdering rival gangsters. The film did a fine job in recreating their childhood home in Bethnal Green, where their doting mother Violet (Billie Whitelaw) lived. The film also used Richmond Theatre, which was transformed into a nightclub for shooting purposes.

The boyhood home of actor Daniel Day-Lewis was in Greenwich. Though born in Kensington, Day-Lewis moved with his family (his father was the Poet Laureate Cecil Day-Lewis and his mother, Jill Balcon, was the daughter of film producer Sir Michael Balcon) to 6 Croom's Hill, Greenwich when he was young. The family remained there for some 15 years, and it was there, in 1970, that Day-Lewis first got a taste for the thespian world. Director John Schlesinger was shooting a scene for **Sunday, Bloody Sunday** (1971) in Greenwich and was looking for local kids as extras. A shopkeeper recommended Day-Lewis and his friends, and, apart from earning £5 for their day's work, Day-Lewis also got his first taste of acting and movies. *Sunday, Bloody Sunday* shot in Greenwich Park and around the area.

WOOLWICH

Michelangelo Antonioni's **Blow Up** (1966), which featured the casting of David Hemmings, Vanessa Redgrave, Sarah Miles and Jane Birkin, is one of those 1960s films that has made the transition from trendy thriller to cult classic. Hemmings plays a fashion photographer who takes photographs of a young couple he spots canoodling in a park, and also inadvertently takes the picture of a corpse partly hidden in the park. The photographs lead him to a woman (Vanessa Redgrave) who wants the pictures, and when he begins to think the photographs might reveal a murder, he returns to the park to investigate, only to find the body has vanished.

Antonioni used Maryon Park off the Woolwich Road in the film, and the spot is still something of a cult venue for fans of the film. Filming also took place in west London and around Holland Park. The film's production designer Assheton Gorton commented: 'We started looking for locations based on a treatment, and as we found the locations we took the director around. He then wrote the script into the locations, and I think that is one of the reasons it works so well. We found this park out in Woolwich: Maryon Park. A very extraordinary park with a sort of hill in the middle surrounded by big tower blocks, right on a bend in the Thames.

'We also had to have somewhere that would service a scene with an antiques shop on the edge of the park, and we were lucky. There was a place there that we took over and converted into an antiques shop,' he added.

Woolwich Arsenal is regularly used by film-makers. Richard Loncraine's acclaimed adaptation of Shakespeare's *Richard III* (1995) shot there, as did Philip Noyce's **The Saint** (1997) with Val Kilmer, Stuart Urban's **Preaching to the Perverted** (1997), **The Leading Man** (1996), which starred Jon Bon Jovi and Thandie Newton, and **Keep the Aspidistra Flying** (1997), starring Richard E. Grant and Helena Bonham Carter. Towards the end of the wartime romantic drama **Charlotte Gray** (2001), Charlotte (Cate Blanchett) has returned from her spying mission in France and is helping out at a London bombsite, assisting Londoners who have lost homes during the Blitz. The scene of the bombsite, with the crashed buses and firemen spraying water over the site, was shot at Woolwich Arsenal.

'**We** found this park out in Woolwich: Maryon Park. A very extraordinary park with a sort of hill in the middle surrounded by big tower blocks, right on a bend in the Thames.'

ASSHETON GORTON, PRODUCTION DESIGNER, *BLOW UP*

Opposite top: *Romance on the Thamesmead Estate in* Beautiful Thing *(1995).*

Opposite: *Alex and his 'Droogs' beat up a tramp in* A Clockwork Orange *(1971).*

THAMESMEAD

An enjoyable low-budget comedy about a burgeoning gay relationship **Beautiful Thing** (1995) used the Thamesmead Estate as the location for much of its filming. Hettie Macdonald's film (based on Jonathan Harvey's play) is a feel-good film with a great Mama Cass soundtrack. It also shot at nearby Lakeside Social Club, Southmere Lake and the Tavy Bridge Piazza, and used other south-east London locations such as the Anchor Pub in Rotherhithe and the Gloucester Arms pub on King William Walk, Greenwich.

Stanley Kubrick's futuristic drama **A Clockwork Orange** (1971) also used Thamesmead and it is in the subway behind the area's Tavy Bridge Shopping Centre that Alex (Malcolm McDowell) and his 'Droogs' attack a tramp.

LONDON LOCATIONS: COMMEMORATIVE PLAQUES

Series of commemorative plaques can be found on the exteriors of a number of London buildings, some famous and distinctive, others simple houses or flats. The plaques denote the homes or workplaces of famous and historical figures and are placed by a variety of organizations.

The first official plaques were erected by the Royal Society of Arts in 1867, with the scheme later taken on by the London County Council in 1901 and the Greater London Council (GLC) in 1965. After the GLC was disbanded, English Heritage began erecting plaques, usually following the scheme of white lettering against a blue backdrop. Local authorities and private individuals have also erected plaques since the early 1900s, as have various entertainment and film bodies, such as the British Film Institute, Comic Heritage and The Dead Comics' Society.

Acres, Birt (1854–1918)
19 Park Road, Barnet (Cinema 100)
Born in America, but resident in Barnet from 1892, Birt Acres was an inventor and pioneer cameraman. He made photographic plates, and at this address he produced, in 1895, what is acknowledged to be the first British movie film.

Baird, John Logie (1888–1946)
3 Crescent Wood Road, Sydenham, SE26 (Greater London Council); 22 Frith Street, W1 (London County Council); 132–5 Long Acre, WC2 (The Royal Television Society)
The Scottish engineer who first developed television and whose later research included producing three-dimensional images, stereophonic sound and screen projection. Baird lived at the first address; first demonstrated television at the second address in 1926; and broadcast the UK's first television programme from the third address, on September 30, 1929. Baird went on to make the first transatlantic television transmission and to demonstrate colour television.

Baker, Hylda (1905–86)
Brinsworth House, Staines Road, Twickenham (Comic Heritage)
Born in Lancashire, Hylda Baker went on to be one of the country's best-loved comedy actresses. She regularly appeared on television, and her films included *Saturday Night and Sunday Morning* (1960), *Up the Junction* (1967) and *Oliver!* (1968). Baker retired to this home for showbusiness folk.

Balcon, Sir Michael (1896–1977)
57a Tufton Street, W1 (Westminster City Council)
The acclaimed British film producer, who made some of the Britain's best comedies, lived here from 1927 to 1939. Balcon's films included *The Lavender Hill Mob* (1951) and *Kind Hearts and Coronets* (1949).

Bliss, Sir Arthur (1891–1975)
East Heath Lodge, 1 East Heath Road, NW3 (English Heritage)
The successful British composer lived at this address between 1929 and 1939. Bliss wrote orchestral, operatic, chamber and film music and was music director of the BBC in 1942–4.

Buchanan, Jack (1890–1957)
44 Mount Street, W1 (Private)
An elegant actor, dancer, film producer and director, Jack Buchanan was one of Britain's most popular performers in the 1930s and 1940s, specializing in light comedy. His films include *Monte Carlo* (1930), *The Gang's All Here* (1939) and *The Band Wagon* (1953), in which he danced alongside Fred Astaire. Buchanan was once resident at this address.

Chaplin, Charlie (Sir Charles Spencer) (1889–1977)
277 Walworth Road, SE17 (Southwark Council); 287 Kennington Road, SE11 (Vauxhall Society); 39 Methley Street, SE11 (The Dead Comics Society)
The much–loved comedian, the son of music-hall entertainers, was born in East Lane, Walworth (the first address) and went on to live at the other addresses before heading off to Hollywood in 1914 where he found fame and fortune.

Coward, Sir Noël Pierce (1899–1973)
17 Gerald Road, SW1 (Private); 131 Waldegrave Road, Teddington (English Heritage); 56 Lenham Road, Sutton (Borough of Sutton)
The English actor, playwright and composer was born at the Teddington address and lived at the others. He starred in several films, including *Our Man in Havana* (1960) and *The Italian Job* (1969), and produced and wrote many others, including *In Which We Serve* (1942), for which he received a special Academy Award, and *Brief Encounter* (1945).

Delfont, Sir Bernard, Baron Delfont of Stepney (Boris Winogradsky) (1909–94)
Prince of Wales Theatre, Coventry Street, W1 (Comic Heritage)
Born in Russia, he was brought to England in 1912 with his older brother, Sir Lew Grade. Both Delfont and Grade were dancers as young men. Delfont moved on to theatre management and was involved with cinema and television interests.

Donat, Robert (1905–58)
8 Meadway, NW11 (English Heritage)
This talented English film and stage actor lived here. Donat's great films include *The 39 Steps* (1935), *Goodbye Mr Chips* (1939), for which he received an Oscar for Best Actor, and *Inn of the Sixth Happiness* (1960).

Evans, Dame Edith (1888–1976)
109 Ebury Street, SW1 (English Heritage)
A classically trained English actress who found fame on stage in both London and New York. During later life she found additional fame after appearing in various films, including *The Importance of Being Earnest* (1952) and *Tom Jones* (1963). Evans was once resident at this address.

Fields, Dame Gracie (Gracie Stansfield) (1898–1979)
20 Frognal Way, Hampstead, NW3 (Heath and old Hampstead Society)
Born in Lancashire, Fields began as a child performer and later found fame in music hall. Her films include *Sally in Our Alley* (1931) and *Sing As We Go* (1934). Fields had this house designed and built in 1934.

Gainsborough Film Studios
Poole Street, N1 (Borough of Hackney)
Site of the famous canal-side film studios, which was home to many great films during its 25 years (1924–49) of activity. Among the many talents who worked at the studio were Alfred Hitchcock, Margaret Lockwood, Gracie Fields and Ivor Novello. More recently it has been converted into housing, though some studio space is still retained.

Hancock, Tony (Anthony John) (1924–68)
10 Grey Close, NW11 (The Dead Comics Society); Teddington Studios, Broom Road, Teddington (Comic Heritage)
This lugubrious comedian lived in Grey Close for a time (1947–8), and worked a great deal at Teddington Studios. Hancock is best remembered for his radio show *Hancock's Half Hour* and later work on television and in the movies.

Handl, Irene (1901–87)
Teddington Studios, Broom Road, Teddington (Comic Heritage)
This English comedy actress worked on television (in her series *For the Love of Ada*), stage, radio and in cinema. Her films include *I'm All Right, Jack* (1959) and *The Italian Job* (1969).

Hepworth, Cecil (1874–1953)
17 Somerset Gardens, SE13 (British Film Institute)
The pioneering British filmmaker was born at this site. In 1905 he made the

early film *Rescued by Rover*, and though later leaving the film business in the 1920s, he made several films for the Ministry of Agriculture during the Second World War.

Hill, Benny (1924–92)
1 and 3 Queen's Gate, SW7 (The Dead Comics Society); Teddington Studios, Broom Road, Teddington (Comic Heritage)
This popular English comedian's fame came mainly from his hit television series *The Benny Hill Show*, but he also featured in several films, notably *The Italian Job* (1969). Hill lived at Queen's Gate from 1960 to 1986, and worked a great deal at Teddington Studios.

Hitchcock, Sir Alfred Joseph (1899–1980)
517 Leytonstone High Road, E11 (Borough of Waltham Forest)
The acclaimed director was born near this site (it is now a petrol station). His early British films include *Blackmail* (1929), *The 39 Steps* (1935) and *The Lady Vanishes* (1939, shot at Gainsborough Studios). He later moved to Hollywood where he found even greater fame and fortune.

Hope, Bob (Leslie Townes Hope) (born 1903)
44 Craigton Road, Eltham, SE9 (British Film Institute)
Born at this house, Bob Hope was taken to America by his parents at the age of four. He worked in vaudeville as a comedian and dancer, and was later to become one of the world's most popular film comedians.

Howerd, Frankie (Francis Alick Howard) (1922–92)
27 Edwardes Square, W8 (Dead Comics Society)
The English comedian lived here from 1966 to 1992. Howerd found fame as a stand-up comedian and on radio, television and cinema. His television comedy series *Up Pompeii* was also adapted into a film version of the same name in 1971.

Jacques, Hattie (Josephine Edwina Jacques) (1924–80)
67 Eardley Crescent, Earl's Court, SW5 (Comic Heritage)
The much-loved comedy actress lived here between 1945 and 1980. She appeared on television and radio, and was a regular in the *Carry On* films, appearing in 14 of the comedies.

James, Sid (1913–76)
35 Gunnersbury Avenue, Ealing, W5 (The British Comedy Society); Teddington Studios, Broom Road, Teddington (Comic Heritage)
Born in South Africa, Sid James lived at the first address between 1956 and 1963, and worked on many productions shot at Teddington. He appeared in

many films (as well as being a regular on radio and television) and was a mainstay of the popular *Carry On* series of films.

Karloff, Boris (William Henry Pratt) (1887–1969)
36 Forest Hill Road, SE23 (English Heritage)
Born at this address, Karloff also spent his early years here. He moved to the USA in 1908 where he became an actor, appearing on stage and in silent films before making his name as the monster in the 1930s horror classic *Frankenstein* (1931).

Laughton, Charles (1899–1962)
15 Percy Street, W1 (English Heritage)
The stage and film actor lived at this address from 1928 to 1931. Laughton found fame in cinema with such films as *The Private Life of Henry VIII* (1932, for which he also received a Best Actor Oscar) and as Quasimodo in *The Hunchback of Notre Dame* (1939).

Leigh, Vivien (Vivien Mary Hartley) (1913–67)
54 Eaton Square, SW1 (English Heritage)
Vivien Leigh made her name in British cinema before moving to the USA where she starred in many major films, including *Gone With the Wind* (1939) and *A Streetcar Named Desire* (1951); she received Oscars for her performances in both films. Leigh was married to Laurence Olivier from 1940 to 1960 and regularly appeared on stage in London with him. She was once resident at this address.

Le Mesurier, John (1912–83)
Barons Keep, Hammersmith, W14 (The Dead Comics Society)
The elegant comedy actor lived at the address from 1966 to 1977. He appeared in many films and was a regular on television, starring as Sergeant Wilson in the much-loved comedy series *Dad's Army* (1968–77).

Lowe, Arthur (1915–82)
2 Maida Avenue, W2 (The Dead Comics Society)
A star of comedy, Arthur Lowe lived at the address between 1969 and 1982. He appeared in many films, though found a better niche on television, featuring in episodes of the soap opera *Coronation Street* before taking the lead role of Captain Mainwaring in the comedy series *Dad's Army*.

Lucan, Arthur (Arthur Towle) (1887–1954)
11 Forty Lane, Wembley (Greater London Council)
With his wife Kitty McShane, Arthur Lucan appeared on stage, radio and screen, playing the character of 'Old Mother Riley'. They also appeared in a series of films featuring the character. He was once resident at this address.

Matthews, Jessie (1907–81)
22 Berwick Street, W1 (Westminster City Council)
The popular dancer and actress was born at this site. Matthews started on the stage aged 10, and became a star in the 1920s, later finding popularity in a series of films, mostly musicals.

More, Kenneth (1914–82)
27 Rumbold Road, SW6 (Private)
This popular British actor lived and died at this address. More starred in many British films, including *The Thirty-Nine Steps* (1959) and *Genevieve* (1953).

Morecambe, Eric (Eric Bartholomew) (1926–84)
85 Torrington Park, N12 (Comic Heritage); Teddington Studios, Broom Road, Teddington (Comic Heritage)
The hilarious English comedian took his stage name from his birthplace of Morecambe in Lancashire, but lived at the first address between 1956 and 1961. During his long partnership with fellow comedian Ernie Wise, he regularly recorded television programmes at Teddington; the pair also starred in a series of films.

Muybridge, Eadweard (1830–1904)
2 Liverpool Road, Kingston (British Film Institute, The Royal Photographic Society)
Eadweard Muybridge was the adopted name of acclaimed photographer Edward James Muggeridge, a pioneer in early motion photography. A famous series of his photographs proved that when a horse gallops there are times when all its hooves leave the ground. Muybridge also invented a device for showing his photographs as moving pictures. He lived at this address from 1894 until his death in 1904.

Neagle, Dame Anna (Marjorie Robertson) (1904–86)
63-4 Park Lane, W1 (Westminster City Council)
The popular actress lived at this address from 1950 until 1964. Neagle appeared on stage and in films, starring in *The Lady with the Lamp* (1951) and *Odette* (1950).

Novello, Ivor (born David Ivor Davies) (1893–1951)
11 Aldwych, WC2 (Greater London Council)
The Welsh-born actor-composer-dramatist lived and died in a flat on the top floor of this building. Novello first appeared on stage in 1921, and his songs included *Keep the Home Fires Burning* (1914), which was one of the most popular songs of the First World War. He also appeared in several films, including *The Lodger* (1926 and the remake in 1932) and *Bonnie Prince Charlie* (1923).

Orton, Joe (1933–67)
25 Noel Road, N1 (Islington Borough Council)
Playwright and screenwriter Joe Orton lived and was murdered here by his lover Kenneth Halliwell, who afterwards committed suicide. His plays (which were also adapted into films) include *Loot* (1966) and *What the Butler Saw* (1968).

Paul, Robert William (1869–1943)
14 Percy Street, W1 (British Film Institute)
The pioneering film producer and director lived here (1914–20), and started a studio near the site in 1895. He filmed the Derby in 1896 and the Oxford and Cambridge Boat Race in 1895.

Python, Monty
Neals Yard, WC2 (Animation Lighting and Recording Studios)
According to the plaque, 'Monty Python' lived at the address 1967–87. In actual fact it marks the location of the studios where the comedy series *Monty Python's Flying Circus* was produced at the time. The Monty Python team went on to make a series of successful films.

Reed, Sir Carol (1906–76)
213 King's Road, SW3 (Private)
The acclaimed film director and producer lived here from 1948 until his death in 1976. Reed's films include classics such as *Odd Man Out* (1947), *The Fallen Idol* (1948) and *The Third Man* (1949). He won an Oscar for the musical *Oliver!* (1968).

Sellers, Peter (1925–80)
10 Muswell Hill Road, N6 (The Dead Comics Society)
The great comic actor Peter Sellers lived here as a boy from 1936 to 1940. He appeared on radio in *The Goon Show*, and from the 1950s onwards starred in a series of comedy films, notably the 'Pink Panther' series of films in which he played the bumbling French detective Inspector Clouseau.

Stewart, Donald Ogden (1894–1980)
103 Frognal Way, Hampstead, NW3 (Hampstead Plaque Fund)
The American–born screenwriter and playwright lived at the address when he retired to England in the 1950s. He won an Oscar for his screenplay of *The Philadelphia Story* (1940), and other films include *The Barratts of Wimpole Street* (1934) and *Cass Timberlaine* (1947).

Tandy, Jessica (1909–94)
58a Geldeston Road, E5 (Borough of Hackney)
Born at this address, Jessica Tandy became a stage and film actress who later

relocated to the USA. She appeared in many films and was a star on stage in both London and New York, though she gained most fame aged 82 when she won a Best Actress Oscar for her performance in *Driving Miss Daisy* (1989).

Tate, Harry (Ronald MacDonald Hutchinson) (1872–1940)
27 Camden Road, Sutton (Borough of Sutton); 72 Longley Road, SW17 (Greater London Council)
Born in Scotland, Harry Tate found great fame as a music-hall performer and star in early silent films. He lived at Camden House between 1920 and 1931, which stood close to the first address, and he also lived at the second address.

Thomas, Terry (Thomas Terry Hoar Stevens) (1911–90)
11 Queensgate Mews, SW7 (Comic Heritage)
The gap-toothed comedy actor lived here from 1949 to 1981. Terry Thomas was a regular on radio and television, and starred in a variety of great comedy films including *School for Scoundrels* (1960) and *Those Magnificent Men in their Flying Machines* (1965).

Thorndike, Dame Sybil (1882–1976)
6 Carlyle Square, SW3 (English Heritage)
The classically trained actress lived here with her husband and family between 1921 and 1932. Thorndike appeared on stage, and later appeared in some 18 movies, including *Nicholas Nickleby* (1947) and *Gone to Earth* (1950).

Wilcox, Herbert (1890–1977)
63–4 Park Lane, W1 (Westminster City Council)
Producer and director Herbert Wilcox (married to Dame Anna Neagle) lived here from 1950 to 1964. His films include *Brewster's Millions* (1935) and *Odette* (1950).

Williams, Kenneth (1926–88)
Marlborough House, Osnaburgh Street, NW1 (The Dead Comics Society)
The London-born comedian and actor was a regular on television and radio; he later found fame as a regular performer in the *Carry On* series of films. Williams was resident at this address from 1972 until his death in 1988.

PUBS, BARS, RESTAURANTS & HOTELS

Why not take the opportunity to follow in the footsteps of your favourite actors and directors by visiting the pubs, bars, restaurants and hotels they filmed in? You could choose from a simple pint in one of the many pubs used by film-makers, you could enjoy a good meal in a restaurant whose surroundings will be strangely familiar, or you could even splash out and enjoy a luxury break in The Savoy Hotel or The Ritz.

PUBS, BARS & RESTAURANTS

192, 192 Kensington Park Road, Notting Hill, W11 2ES. Tel: 020 7229 0482. *Bridget Jones's Diary* (2001)

The Anchor Tavern, 34 Bankside, Southwark, SE1 9EF. Tel: 020 7407 1577. *Mission: Impossible* (1996)

Atlantic Bar and Grill, 20 Glasshouse Street, Soho, W1B 5DJ. Tel: 020 7734 4888. *Bring Me the Head of Mavis Davis* (1999)

Battersea Park Café (now called La Gondola al Parco), Battersea Park, SW11. Tel: 020 7352 0113. *Martha, Meet Frank, Daniel and Laurence* (1998)

Bertorelli's, 19–23 Charlotte Street, Fitzrovia, W1P 1HP. Tel: 020 7636 4174. *Sliding Doors* (1998)

Blue Anchor, 13 Lower Mall, Hammersmith, W6 9DJ. Tel: 020 8748 5774. *Sliding Doors* (1998)

Borough Café, 11 Park Street, Southwark, SE1 9AQ. Tel: 020 7407 5048. *Keep the Aspidistra Flying* (1998)

Café de Paris, 3 Coventry Street, Soho, W1D 6BL. Tel: 020 7734 7700. *Gangster No. 1* (2000)

Cantina del Ponte, 36c Shad Thames, Southwark SE1 2YE. Tel: 020 7403 5403. *Bridget Jones's Diary* (2001)

The City Barge, 27 Strand-on-the-Green, Chiswick, W4 3PH. Tel: 020 8994 2148. *Help!* (1965)

The Cock Tavern, The Poultry Market, Smithfield Central Markets, EC1A 9LH. Tel: 020 7248 2918. *Gangster No. 1* (2000)

Coins Coffee House (now called Cash Bar), 105–107 Talbot Road, Notting Hill, W11 2AT. Tel: 020 7221 8099. *Bedrooms and Hallways* (1998)

Crocker's Folly, 24 Aberdeen Place, Maida Vale, NW8 8JR. Tel: 020 7286 6608. *Reds* (1981)

Dinos, 1 Pelham Street, South Kensington, SW7 2ND. Tel: 020 7589 3511. *Repulsion* (1965)

Earl of Warwick (now called Golborne House), 36 Golborne Road, North Kensington, W10 5PR. Tel: 020 8960 6260. *East is East* (1999)

Dôme Restaurant (now called Café Rouge), 34 Wellington Street, Covent Garden, WC2E 7BD. Tel: 020 7836 0998. *Four Weddings and a Funeral* (1994)

The Globe, 37 Bow Street, WC2. *Frenzy* (1972)

Hakkasan, 8 Hanway Place, W1P 9HD. Tel: 020 7927 7000. *About a Boy* (2002)

Holly Bush, 22 Holly Mount, Hampstead, NW3 6SG. Tel: 020 7435 2892. *The Killing of Sister George* (1968)

The Lamb Tavern, 10–12 Leadenhall Market, EC3V 1LR. Tel: 020 7626 2454. *Brannigan* (1975)

Lamb and Flag, 33 Rose Street, Covent Garden, WC2E 9EB. Tel: 020 7497 9504. *Travels With My Aunt* (1972)

Lowndes Arms, 33 Chesham Street, Belgravia, SW1X 8NQ. Tel: 020 7235 4437. *The Crying Game* (1992)

Mas Café (now called Manor), 6–8 All Saint's Road, Notting Hill, W11 1HH. Tel: 020 7243 6363. *Sliding Doors* (1998)

Mike's Cafe, 12 Blenheim Crescent, W11. Tel: 020 7229 3757. *Martha, Meet Frank, Daniel and Laurence* (1998)

Newman Arms, 23 Rathbone Street, W1P 1AG. Tel: 020 7636 1127. *Peeping Tom* (1960)

Nobu, at The Metropolitan Hotel, Old Park Lane, W1Y 4LB. Tel: 020 7447 1047. *Notting Hill* (1999)

Otto's, Sutherland Avenue, W9. Tel: 020 7266 3131. *About a Boy* (2002)

Pharmacy, 150 Notting Hill Gate, Notting Hill, W11 3QG. Tel: 020 7221 2442. *Bridget Jones's Diary* (2001)

Pitcher and Piano, 59–70 Dean Street, Soho, W1. Tel: 020 7434 3585. *Wonderland* (1998)

Royal Standard, 67 Pelton Road, Greenwich, SE10. Tel: 020 8293 0687. *Love is the Devil* (1998)

The Salisbury, 90 St Martin's Lane, WC2. Tel: 020 7836 5683. *Travels With My Aunt* (1972); *Victim* (1961)

Simpson's-in-the-Strand, 100 The Strand, WC2R 0EW. Tel: 020 7836 9112. *The Duellists* (1977); Howards End (1992)

Turk's Head, 28 Winchester Road, St Margaret's, Twickenham, TW1 4LL. Tel: 020 8891 1852. *A Hard Day's Night* (1964)

Vic Naylor's, 38–40 St John Street, Clerkenwell, EC1M 4AY. Tel: 020 7608 2181. *Lock, Stock and Two Smoking Barrels* (1998)

The Warwick Castle, 225 Portobello Road, Notting Hill, W11 1LU. *I Hired a Contract Killer* (1990)

Wimpy Bar, 251a Southwark Park Road, SE16 3TS. Tel: 020 7237 4140. *Nil By Mouth* (1997)

The Wishing Well, 79 Chaumert Road, East Dulwich, SE15. Tel: 020 7639 5052. *Last Orders* (2001)

HOTELS

Blake's Hotel, 33 Roland Gardens, SW7 3PF. Tel: 020 7370 6701. *Martha, Meet Frank, Daniel and Laurence* (1998)

Le Meridien Grosvenor Hotel, 86–90 Park Lane W1K 7TN. Tel: 020 7499 6363. *Sexy Beast* (2000)

Halcyon Hotel, 81 Holland Park Avenue, Holland Park, W11 3RZ. Tel: 020 7727 7288. *The Saint* (1997)

Hempel Hotel, 31–35 Craven Hill Gardens, Bayswsater, W2 3EA. Tel: 020 7298 9000. *Notting Hill* (1999)

Marlborough Hotel, Bloomsbury Street, Bloomsbury, WC1B 3QD. Tel: 020 7636 5601. Shirley Valentine (1989)

The Park Lane Hotel, Piccadilly, W1Y 8BX. Tel: 020 7499 6321. *Gangster No. 1* (2000)

The Ritz Hotel, 150 Piccadilly, W1V 9DG. Tel: 020 7493 8181. *Dinner at the Ritz* (1937); *Modesty Blaise* (1966); *Notting Hill* (1999)

Royal Eagle Hotel, 26–30 Craven Road, Bayswater W2 3QB. Tel: 020 7706 0700. *Trainspotting* (1996)

St Ermine's, Caxton Street, Westminster, SW1H 0QW. Tel: 020 7222 7888. *The Importance of Being Earnest* (2002)

The Savoy Hotel, The Strand, WC2R 0EU. Tel: 020 7836 4343. *Notting Hill* (1999); *Entrapment* (1999); *The Long Good Friday* (1980)

Thistle Tower Hotel, St Katherine's Way, EW1 1LD. Tel: 020 7481 2575. *Spiceworld: The Movie* (1997)

Le Meridien Waldorf Hotel, Aldwych, WC2B 4DD. Tel: 020 7836 2400. *Another Life* (1999)

LONDON...
BUT NOT LONDON

London is a diverse, sprawling city and almost every corner of it has appeared in a movie at some time over the past hundred years. However, London doesn't always appear as London, rather it is occasionally used to recreate more far-flung places, such as the grand buildings of St Petersburg, war-torn Vietnam and, on numerous occasions, the city of New York from the 18th century to today.

🎥 *Death Wish III* (1985
Lambeth Hospital was used as the New York Bronx.

🎥 *Empire of the Sun* (1987)
Beckton Gas Works in Docklands was used for the interiors of a Japanese internment camp.

🎥 *Eyes Wide Shut* (1999)
Berners Street and Eastcastle Street in Soho doubled as New York's Greenwich Village, while the Berners Street club Madame Jo-Jo's became New York jazz venue Club Sonata.

🎥 *Full Metal Jacket* (1987)
Beckton Gas Works in Docklands doubled as a war-torn town in Vietnam.

🎥 *GoldenEye* (1995)
Somerset House in the West End became St Petersburg.

🎥 *The Hunger* (1983)
The nightclub Heaven, at Charing Cross, became a New York nightclub, and the Senate House at University College a New York clinic.

🎥 *Indiana Jones and the Last Crusade* (1989)
The Royal Horticultural Hall in Westminster doubled as Berlin airport as Indy makes his escape from Germany.

🎥 *A Kiss Before Dying* (1991)
The First National Bank of Chicago at 90 Long Acre, Covent Garden, doubles as the Philadelphia police headquarters.

🎞 Mission: Impossible (1996)
The foyer of County Hall on the South Bank became the CIA headquarters and the entrance to Tate Britain became a Czech embassy.

🎞 Mrs Dalloway (1997)
Cornhill in the City doubled as 1940s Bond Street, while Walthamstow Town Hall became a period American building.

🎞 Patriot Games (1992)
The Royal Naval College in Greenwich became the White House in Washington.

🎞 Quills (2000)
The Royal Naval College in Greenwich became Napoleon's home.

🎞 Reds (1981)
Crocker's Folly pub in Maida Vale doubled as the New York Writer's Club, while Somerset House in the West End became a building attacked by Bolshevik revolutionaries.

🎞 The Saint (1997)
Camden Town Hall doubled as the American Embassy in Moscow, the Royal Horticultural Hall in Westminster became Berlin airport and Woolwich Arsenal became a Russian palace.

🎞 Shining Through (1992)
Aldwych and Kingsway acted as New York, St Pancras as Zurich and the Royal Naval College in Greenwich as the Pentagon.

🎞 Sleepy Hollow (1999)
Somerset House doubled as 1780s New York.

🎞 Spy Game (2001)
Robert Redford drives his nifty Porsche through Regent's Park rather than the countryside of Virginia on his way to CIA headquarters.

🎞 Superman IV: The Quest for Peace (1987)
Aldwych Underground station doubled as the New York underground.

🎞 Titanic Town (1998)
Hackney Road in Shoreditch was transformed into the Belfast of 1972 for a scene in this drama with Julie Walters as a Catholic housewife who tries to bring peace to the region.

BOLLYWOOD IN LONDON

Britain is increasingly becoming a popular location shoot for Bollywood movies, with directors favouring the castles and glens of Scotland, the plentiful stately homes and – naturally enough – the iconic landmarks of London. Yash Chopra and his director son, Aditya, have made several successful Bollywood films in London, and the trend looks set to run and run. Most Bollywood films set in London go out of their way to ensure their audiences get a real tourist-journey through the city, often from the view of an open-top bus, with the famous buildings and landmarks serving as a backdrop to the music and action, rather than appearing as extensive locations.

🎥 *Chaand Kaa Tukdaa* (1994)
Directed by Saawan Kumar. Starring: Sridevi, Salman Khan, Aishwarya Rai.
LOCATIONS: Big Ben, Houses of Parliament, Parliament Square, Tower Bridge, Piccadilly Circus, Oxford Street, Buckingham Palace, Canary Wharf, Docklands, London City Airport.

🎥 *Dil Ne Phir Yaad Kiya* (2001)
Directed by Rajat Rawail. Starring: Govinda, Tabu, Jackie Shroff, Pooja Batra.
LOCATIONS: Big Ben, Houses of Parliament, Tower Bridge, Trafalgar Square, Buckingham Palace.

🎥 *Dilwale Dulhania Le Jayenge* (1995)
Directed by Aditya Chopra. Starring: Shah Rukh Khan, Kajol, Amrish Puri.
LOCATIONS: (mainly via an open-top bus tour) Big Ben, Houses of Parliament, Whitehall, Westminster Bridge, South Bank, Tower Bridge, Trafalgar Square, Leicester Square, Buckingham Palace, King's Cross station, Angel Underground station, the Broadway in Southall.

🎥 *Dulhan Banoo Mein Teri* (2000)
Directed by B Subhash. Starring: Faraaz Khan, Deepti Bhatnagar, Kashmira Shah.
LOCATIONS: Tower Bridge, Trafalgar Square, Leicester Square, Piccadilly Circus, India House, Docklands.

🎥 *Hero Hindustani* (1998)
Directed by Aziz Sajawal. Starring: Arshad Warsi, Namrata Shirodkar.
LOCATIONS: Big Ben, Houses of Parliament, South Bank, Cleopatra's Needle, Tower Bridge, Trafalgar Square, Piccadilly Circus, Plaza shopping centre on Oxford Street, Portland Place, Westminster Cathedral, Natural History Museum.

Jaanan Samjha Karo (1999)
Directed by Andaleb M. Sultanpuri. Starring: Salman Khan, Urmila Matondkar, Monica Bedi.
LOCATIONS: (mainly by open-top bus tour) Big Ben, Houses of Parliament, Oxo Tower, Tower Bridge, Piccadilly Circus, Hamleys toy store on Regent Street, Harrods, Feltham Megabowl, Acton Royale Leisure Park.

Jayam Manadera (2000)
Directed by M. Shankar. Starring: Venkatesh, Soundarya, Bhanupriya.
LOCATIONS: (open-top bus tour again) Houses of Parliament, Westminster Abbey, Westminster Bridge, British Airways London Eye, London Bridge, Tower of London, Trafalgar Square, Piccadilly Circus, Buckingham Palace, Albert Memorial.

Kabhi Khushi Kabhie Gham (2001)
Directed by: Karan Johar. Starring: Amitabh Bachchan, Jaya Bachchan, Shah Rukh Khan.
LOCATIONS: Tower Bridge, Butler's Wharf.

Kuch Khatti Kuch Meethi (2001)
Directed by: Rahul Rawail. Starring: Rishi Kapoor, Rati Agnihotri, Sunil Shetty.
LOCATIONS: British Airways London Eye, Tower Bridge, Tower of London, Edgware, Regency Club.

Lamhe (1991)
Directed by Yash Chopra. Starring: Anil Kapoor, Sridevi, Waheedha Rehman, Anupam Kher.
LOCATIONS: Trafalgar Square, Regent's Park, Whiteley's Shopping Centre in Bayswater.

Main Solah Baras Ki (1998)
Directed by Dev Anand. Starring: Dev Anand, Sabrina, Jas Arora, Neeru.
LOCATIONS: Big Ben, Houses of Parliament, Westminster Bridge, South Bank, Trafalgar Square, Leicester Square, Piccadilly Circus, Buckingham Palace.

Yaadein (2001)
Directed by Subhash Ghai. Starring: Hrithik Roshan, Kareena Kapoor, Kackie Shroff.
LOCATIONS: Big Ben, Houses of Parliament, Whitehall, Tower Bridge, Leicester Square.

BIBLIOGRAPHY & FURTHER READING

BOOKS

Movie Locations: A Guide to the UK and Ireland Mark Adams (Boxtree, 2000)
The Worldwide Guide to Movie Locations Tony Reeves (Titan Books, 2003)
The Movie Traveller Allan Foster (Polygon, 2000)
London on Film Colin Sorensen (Museum of London, 1996)
Discovering London Plaques Derek Sumeray (Shire Books, 1999)
Time Out – London Walks Volume 1 (Penguin, 2001)
NFT50: A Celebration of Fifty Years of the National Film Theatre (BFI Publishing)
The Macmillan International Film Encyclopedia Ephrain Katz (Macmillan, 2001)
An Autobiography of British Cinema Brian McFarlane (Methuen/BFI Publishing, 1997)
Hitchcock at Work Bill Krohn (Phanes Press, 2000)
British Stars and Stardom editor Bruce Babington (Manchester University Press, 2001)
Alexander Korda Karol Kulik (Virgin, 1991)
The "Carry On Companion" Robert Ross (B T Batsford, 1998)
Check Book 4: The British Film Commission (British Film Commission)
Notting Hill Richard Curtis (Coronet, 1999)
On Location: The Film Fan's Guide to Britain and Ireland Brian Pendreigh (Mainstream Publishing, 1995)
"Radio Times" Guide to Films: 2003 (Radio Times, 2002)

MAGAZINES

The Hollywood Reporter
Movieline
Premiere
Screen International
Sight & Sound
Variety

WEBSITE

www.imdb.com – the Internet Movie Data Base (IMDB).

INDEX

Page numbers in *italic* refer to maps

A
The Abominable Dr Phibes 59, 66
About a Boy 20–21, 32, *41*, 44–5, *59*, 66–7, *129*, 132
Absolute Beginners 114, 118
Acres, Birt 154
Acton 103
Afraid of the Dark 97, 98
Albert Bridge 117–18
Alexander Palace 81–2
Alfie 47, 52, *59*, 60, *88–9*, 96, *122*, 124
Alfredos 162
Ali G Indahouse 108, 108–9, *129*, 133
Aliens 102, 103
An American Werewolf in London 20–21, 23, 34, *59*, 67, 97, *98*
The Anchor Tavern 162
Angels and Insects 137, 139
Anne of the Thousand Days 129, 132
Another Life 20–21, 23
Arabesque 13, 14–15, 20–21, 25, *59*, 67
Around the World in Eighty Days 20–21, 34, *108–9*, 112, *114*, 118
Arsenal 79–80
The Arsenal Stadium Mystery 77, 79
Atlantic Bar and Grill 162
The Avengers 14–15, 16–17, 20–21, 26, 35, *47*, 49, 108, *108–9*, *114*, 117, *149*, 150
The Awakening 14, 14–15

B
B Monkey 114, 116
Babymother 70, 70–1
Backbeat 58, 59, 63
Baird, John Logie 154
Baker, Hylda 154
Balcon, Sir Michael 154–5

Bank Holiday 136, 137
Barbican 43–4
Barnes 130
Batman 59, 61, 102, 103
Battersea 123–5
Battersea Park Café 162
Battersea Power Sation 124
The Battle of Britain 47, 53
Bayswater 91–2
Bean 108–9, 112, 113, 114
Beat Girls 20–21, 30
Beautiful Thing 149, 153
Beckton 83–4
The Bed Sitting Room 41, 42
Bedazzled 14–15, 18, *20–21*, 34
Bedrooms and Hallways 88–9, 92
Belgravia 112
Bend It Like Beckham 20–21, 34, *102*, 105
Bermondsey 143
Bertorelli's 162
Bethnal Green 54–5
Billion Dollar Brain 59, 60
Billy Elliot 20–21, 22
Billy Liar 59, 68
Bishopsgate 50
Black Beauty 20–21, 25
Blackfriars 40
Blackmail 12
Blake's Hotel 165
Bliss, Sir Arthur 155
Bloomsbury 12–16
Blow Up 149, 152
Blue Anchor 162
Blue Ice 20–21, 30, *137*, 142
Blue Juice 88–9, 90
The Blue Lamp 88–9, 90
Bond Street 37
Born Romantic 13, 14–15, 47, 54, *122*, 128
The Borough 141–2
Borough Café 162
The Borrowers 102, 103
The Bounty 149, 150
The Boy Who Turned Yellow 47, 51, *59*, 64
Bramley Arms 162
Brannigan 20–21, 34, *47*, 49,

51
Brassed off 114, 118–19
Brazil 98, 99
Brent Cross 72
Brentford 104
Bridget Jones's Diary 20–1, 35, *41*, 42, *59*, 62, *88–9*, 94, *137*, 140–41
Brief Encounter 59, 68
Bring Me The Head of Mavis Davis 20–21, 30, *47*, 51
Britannia Hospital 81, 82
British Museum 12–14
Brixton 126–8
Buchanan, Jack 155
Bulldog Jack 14–15, 16
Bunny Lake is Missing 59, 65, *88, 88–9*

C
Café de Paris 163
Café Rouge 163
Caine, Michael 145
Camberwell 146
Camden 62–3
Cantina del Ponte 163
Career Girls 47, 48, *59*, 61
Carrington 149, 150
Carry on at Your Convenience 70–71, 72
Carry on Constable 102, 103
Cash Bar 163
Castaway 98, 99
Chaand Kaa Tukdaa 168
Chaplin 41, 43, *47*, 55, *59*, 61, 76, *77*
Chaplin, Charlie 146, 155
Charlotte Gray 148, 148, 149, 152
Chelsea 116–18
Cheyne Walk 117–18
Children of the Damned 47, 49
A Christmas Carol 149, 150
Circus 88–9, 95
City 38–55
The City Barge 163
The City Bridge 163
Clapham 126
Clerkenwell 44–6

ACKNOWLEDGEMENTS

Mark Adams: 55

Reproduced courtesy of Mark Adams/FilmFour: 27, 33, 36, 71, 80, 121 (top), 123, 127, 152 (top)

BFI: 78, 104

Courtesy of Canal+ Image UK: 7, 12, 17, 30, 31, 40, 50, 58, 96, 110 (BFI), 116, 119, 125, 139, 140, 144

Reproduced courtesy of Carlton International Media Ltd/LFI: 15 (Mark Adams), 40 (BFI), 48 (Mark Adams), 68–9 (BFI), 111 (BFI), 115 (BFI), 136 (BFI)

Chris Coe: 49, 101, 142

The World Is Not Enough © 1999 Danjaq LLC and United Artists Corporation. All rights reserved. 007 Gun Symbol Logo and related James Bond trademarks are trademarks of Danjaq LLC. Licensed by Eon Productions and United Artists Corporation. All rights reserved: 121 (bottom, BFI)

Caroline Jones: 57

Eric Nathan: 63, 75, 95, 135

Four Weddings and a Funeral © 1994 Orion Pictures Corporation. All rights reserved: 19 (Mark Adams)

David Paterson: 4, 11, 13, 22, 23, 25, 26, 29, 32, 34, 39, 42, 44, 46, 51, 52, 60, 64, 87, 105, 107, 117, 130–31, 138, 150

Reproduced Courtesy of Universal Studios Licensing LLLP/BFI: 67, 92–3, 140–41

Reproduced courtesy of Warner Bros.: 84 (BFI), 152 (bottom, Mark Adams)